THE BEDFORD SERIES IN HISTORY AND CULTURE

Jefferson vs. Hamilton

Confrontations That Shaped a Nation

THE BEDFORD SERIES IN HISTORY AND CULTURE

Jefferson vs. Hamilton

Confrontations That Shaped a Nation

Noble E. Cunningham Jr.

University of Missouri, Columbia

BEDFORD/ST. MARTIN'S   Boston   ◆   New York

For Bedford/St. Martin's
Executive Editor for History and Political Science: Katherine E. Kurzman
Developmental Editor: Louise Townsend
Editorial Assistant: Chip Turner
Senior Production Supervisor: Joe Ford
Marketing Manager: Charles Cavaliere
Project Management: Books By Design, Inc.
Index: Books By Design, Inc.
Text Design: Claire Seng-Niemoeller
Cover Design: Richard Emery Design, Inc.
Cover Art: Charles Willson Peale, *Thomas Jefferson* (detail), ca. 1791. Courtesy of Independence National Historical Park. Charles Willson Peale, *Alexander Hamilton* (detail), ca. 1791. Courtesy of Independence National Historical Park.
Composition: G & S Typesetters, Inc.
Printing and Binding: Haddon Craftsmen, an R. R. Donnelley & Sons Company

President: Charles H. Christensen
Editorial Director: Joan E. Feinberg
Director of Marketing: Karen R. Melton
Director of Editing, Design, and Production: Marcia Cohen
Manager, Publishing Services: Emily Berleth

Library of Congress Catalog Card Number: 99-63694

5
f e d c

For information, write: Bedford/St. Martin's, 75 Arlington Street, Boston, MA 02116
(617-399-4000)

ISBN: 0-312-08585-0 (paperback)
0-312-22821-X (hardcover)

Foreword

The Bedford Series in History and Culture is designed so that readers can study the past as historians do.

The historian's first task is finding the evidence. Documents, letters, memoirs, interviews, pictures, movies, novels, or poems can provide facts and clues. Then the historian questions and compares the sources. There is more to do than in a courtroom, for hearsay evidence is welcome, and the historian is usually looking for answers beyond act and motive. Different views of an event may be as important as a single verdict. How a story is told may yield as much information as what it says.

Along the way the historian seeks help from other historians and perhaps from specialists in other disciplines. Finally, it is time to write, to decide on an interpretation and how to arrange the evidence for readers.

Each book in this series contains an important historical document or group of documents, each document a witness from the past and open to interpretation in different ways. The documents are combined with some element of historical narrative—an introduction or a biographical essay, for example—that provides students with an analysis of the primary source material and important background information about the world in which it was produced.

Each book in the series focuses on a specific topic within a specific historical period. Each provides a basis for lively thought and discussion about several aspects of the topic and the historian's role. Each is short enough (and inexpensive enough) to be a reasonable one-week assignment in a college course. Whether as classroom or personal reading, each book in the series provides firsthand experience of the challenge—and fun—of discovering, recreating, and interpreting the past.

Lynn Hunt
David W. Blight
Natalie Zemon Davis
Ernest R. May

Preface

The letters, documents, and other papers from the days of Thomas Jefferson and Alexander Hamilton are extensive, and they are especially rich for the period when both men were serving in President George Washington's administration. The papers reveal how two leading political figures faced the major issues of their day, providing important insights into the founding of the American Republic. This book centers not on the entire lives of Jefferson and Hamilton nor on the full history of their times. Instead, the focus is on their opposing views and actions relating to the emerging American nation, in whose development each man played a critical role.

The differences between Thomas Jefferson and Alexander Hamilton, and the confrontations that accompanied them, did much to shape the early American Republic. The papers of the two influential statesmen broaden an understanding not only of the formative years of the American Republic, but also of the United States today.

Neither a dual biography nor a history of their times, this book offers texts and documents aimed at illuminating the positions that Jefferson and Hamilton took on public issues and their impact on the times. Instead of a separate text and accompanying documents, the documents have been incorporated into the text. The aim has been to provide a broader and clearer understanding of the documents, their authors, and the wider history of which they form a part. By studying excerpts from important and revealing documents from the times in which Jefferson and Hamilton lived, readers may gain new insights into the crucial formative years of the American Republic.

The portraits, paintings, prints, and manuscripts illustrating this book are contemporary with the lives of Thomas Jefferson and Alexander Hamilton.

In printing the documents and manuscripts in this text, original spelling and punctuation have been retained.

ACKNOWLEDGMENTS

I want to thank Charles H. Christensen, Joan E. Feinberg, and Katherine E. Kurzman of Bedford/St. Martin's and Ernest R. May of Harvard University for their interest in this book and their patience in awaiting its completion. I have also profited from the reading of the manuscript by Robert Allison, Janet Coryell, Carl Prince, and Gene Smith. I am greatly indebted to Louise Townsend of Bedford/St. Martin's for her skills in the editing of the manuscript for publication.

Noble E. Cunningham Jr.

Contents

Illustrations

Jefferson vs. Hamilton

Confrontations That Shaped a Nation

Introduction

During the early years of the American Republic following the winning of independence, Thomas Jefferson and Alexander Hamilton were among the most influential men active in the politics and government of the United States. The two men came from widely different backgrounds. Jefferson, the older of the two men, was born into the privileged world of colonial Virginia planters. Hamilton began life in an insecure world in the British West Indies.

For both Jefferson and Hamilton, the American Revolution was a life-defining event, and each man risked his life in that struggle. Jefferson, as the drafter of the Declaration of Independence and the wartime governor of Virginia, and Hamilton, as a young officer on the battlefield, directly faced the dangers of rebellion and war in different roles.

In postwar America, both men gained influential places in the affairs of state. Hamilton was present and active in the Constitutional Convention of 1787 in Philadelphia, where the Constitution of the United States was drafted. Jefferson was then in Paris, serving as the U.S. minister to France. Although Jefferson did not participate in the drafting of the Constitution and would have proposed some changes had he been at the convention, he supported the adoption of the new instrument of national government.

Jefferson and Hamilton had their longest and closest association — and displayed their most important differences — while serving in President George Washington's cabinet. Jefferson, as the first secretary of state, and Hamilton, as the first secretary of the Treasury, were the leading members of President Washington's initial cabinet. With different backgrounds and experiences, the two presidential advisers had opposing visions of the path the young nation should follow. Both men attracted strong supporters whose influence helped to shape the times in which they lived and the future destiny of the United States.

During these years, Hamilton's policies and actions as head of the Treasury Department had a major role in establishing a firm financial base for the new American Republic. In addition to the direction of foreign affairs, Secretary of State Jefferson was charged with all other matters except finances and military affairs. Jefferson retired as secretary of state at the end of 1793; Hamilton remained at the Treasury Department until the end of January 1795.

Hamilton made every effort to prevent Jefferson's election in the contest against John Adams for the presidency in 1800. At a time when each presidential elector voted in the electoral college for two candidates without distinguishing between president and vice president, the electoral vote ended in a tie between Jefferson and Aaron Burr, who was the candidate for vice president. Hamilton then strongly supported the election of Jefferson over Burr, and Jefferson was the winner in the final contest.

In his inaugural address, delivered in the new capital city of Washington on March 4, 1801, Jefferson presented his vision of the new American Republic — a vision that Hamilton did not share. Hamilton's political world now centered in New York State. There, the political contests of that state and Hamilton's rivalry with Aaron Burr led to the tragic duel with Burr that ended Hamilton's life before the close of Jefferson's first term as president. With Alexander Hamilton deceased, no single individual would again so clearly define an agenda to compete with that of Thomas Jefferson.

1

Different Paths to Fame

Thomas Jefferson was born on April 13, 1743, in Albemarle County in the English colony of Virginia. A few years earlier, his father, Peter Jefferson, had obtained one thousand acres along the Rivanna River, and he soon added four hundred more. The land, within sight of the Blue Ridge Mountains, lay on the western edges of settlement, and Jefferson would always retain close ties to the land. Although not one of the largest landholders in the county, his father was a rising young planter and slaveholder, and Jefferson's economic future was secure. So also was Jefferson's social status, for his mother, Jane Randolph, was a member of one of the most influential families in Virginia.

The wealth of his father assured Jefferson the best educational opportunities the colony could provide. His early education began at the age of five under private tutors. At the age of nine, he was enrolled in a Latin school in a neighboring county, and at fourteen he began studies twelve miles from home in a log school run by the well-educated Anglican rector of a nearby parish. After two years of instruction under this classical scholar, Jefferson could read Greek and Roman works in the original.[1]

Alexander Hamilton's early life was strikingly different from Jefferson's. He was born on the British-held island of Nevis in the West Indies, probably on January 11, 1755. His father, James Hamilton, was a Scotsman of prominent family but never successful in his own ventures. His mother, Rachel Fawcett Lavien, had left her husband, John Lavien, and set up a home with James Hamilton. Alexander was the second son of that union. He was eleven years old when the family moved to Saint Croix, where his mother had previously lived. In the same year, his

---

[1] Noble E. Cunningham Jr., *In Pursuit of Reason: The Life of Thomas Jefferson* (Baton Rouge: Louisiana State University Press, 1987), pp. 1–4.

father drifted away. Alexander Hamilton would never see him again, though he had occasional contact with him by mail and in later years would send him money. Hamilton's mother, who had opened a small store on Saint Croix after his father left, died in 1768. Full of hardships and insecurities, Hamilton's early life also lacked educational opportunities. In later years, Hamilton was reticent about his childhood, but it is known that after his mother's death he became a clerk in the firm of Beekman and Cruger in Christiansted, Saint Croix — a firm with close connections in New York. Here Hamilton gained valuable experience in business and finance, and within a few years he was managing the office during Nicholas Cruger's extended absences from Saint Croix.[2]

The security of Jefferson's youth contrasts sharply with the insecurity of Hamilton's early years. Jefferson also experienced the early loss of his father, who died when Jefferson was fourteen. But Hamilton was left on his own after the early death of his mother. Thomas Jefferson's earliest known letter, written in early 1760 at the age of sixteen, concerned his plans to attend the College of William and Mary. Addressed to one of his guardians, the letter revealed an ambitious and industrious youth.

[2]Jacob Ernest Cooke, *Alexander Hamilton* (New York: Charles Scribner's Sons, 1982), pp. 1–3; John C. Miller, *Alexander Hamilton and the Growth of the New Nation* (New York: Harper & Row, 1964), pp. 1–5.

THOMAS JEFFERSON

Letter to John Harvie

January 14, 1760

I was at Colo. Peter Randolph's about a Fortnight ago, and my Schooling falling into Discourse, he said he thought it would be to my Advantage to go to the College, and was desirous I should go, as indeed I am myself for several Reasons. In the first place as long as I stay at the Mountains the Loss of one fourth of my Time is inevitable, by Company's coming here and detaining me from School. And likewise my Absence will in a great Measure put a Stop to so much Company, and by that Means lessen the Expences of the Estate in House-Keeping. And on the other Hand by go-

Julian P. Boyd, Charles T. Cullen, and John Catanzariti, eds., *The Papers of Thomas Jefferson,* 27 vols. to date (Princeton: Princeton University Press, 1950–), 1:3.

ing to the College I shall get a more universal Acquaintance, which may hereafter be serviceable to me; and I suppose I can pursue my Studies in the Greek and Latin as well there as here, and likewise learn something of the Mathematics. I shall be glad of your opinion.

Jefferson argued his case convincingly, and in the spring of 1760 he enrolled in the College of William and Mary in Williamsburg. He later looked back and saw his study there as one of the major transforming experiences of his life:

> It was my great fortune, and what probably fixed the destinies of my life, that Dr. William Small of Scotland was then professor of Mathematics, a man profound in most of the useful branches of science, with a happy talent of communication, correct and gentlemanly manners, and an enlarged and liberal mind. He, most happily for me, became soon attached to me and made me his daily companion when not engaged in the school; and from his conversation I got my first views of the expansion of science and of the system of things in which we are placed.[3]

The earliest known letter of Alexander Hamilton, penned in November 1769, when he was fourteen, like Jefferson's letter, concerned future ambitions. Written to a friend, Edward Stevens, who had been sent by his father, Thomas Stevens, to study at King's College in New York, Hamilton seemed as eager to leave Saint Croix as Jefferson had been to get away from Albemarle County.

[3] Jefferson, Autobiography, in Paul L. Ford, ed., *The Works of Thomas Jefferson,* Federal Edition, 12 vols. (New York: G. P. Putnam's Sons, 1904), 1:5–6.

ALEXANDER HAMILTON
Letter to Edward Stevens
November 11, 1769

. . . my Ambition is prevalent that I contemn the grov'ling and condition of a Clerk or the like, to which my Fortune, &c. condemns me and would

---

Harold C. Syrett et al., eds., *The Papers of Alexander Hamilton,* 27 vols. (New York: Columbia University Press, 1961–87), 1:4.

willing risk my life tho' not my Character to exalt my Station. Im confident, Ned that my Youth excludes me from any hopes of immediate Preferment nor do I desire it, but I mean to prepare the way for futurity. Im no Philosopher you see and may be jusly said to Build Castles in the Air. My Folly makes me ashamd and beg youll Conceal it, yet Neddy we have seen such Schemes successfull when the Projector is Constant I shall Conclude saying I wish there was a War.

Early on, Hamilton thus saw war as a way to advance. Later, the American Revolution would give him that opportunity.

Hamilton's early ambitions to improve his lot in life were largely made possible by Nicholas Cruger, Thomas Stevens, the Reverend Hugh Knox, and others on Saint Croix who raised funds to enable him to go to the mainland to further his education.[4] The exact date when Hamilton sailed from Saint Croix is unknown. The most convincing scholarly speculation is that Hamilton arrived in New York Harbor during June 1773.[5] He would never return to Saint Croix.

At the time the eighteen-year-old Hamilton arrived in New York, Thomas Jefferson, then thirty, had been practicing law for more than six years. He had married Martha Wayles Skelton on January 1, 1782, and they were already living at Monticello, the house — then under construction — that would become his home for the rest of his life. Earlier, in 1765, as a student in Williamsburg, Jefferson had heard Patrick Henry deliver his famous speech against the Stamp Act. A member of the Virginia House of Burgesses since 1769, Jefferson joined a group of young members who were vigorous in asserting the rights of the colony within the British Empire.

Virginia remained quiet at the beginning of the 1770s after the British Parliament repealed all of the Townshend duties except that on tea. Nevertheless, concerns about colonial rights were rising sharply when the Virginia Assembly met in March 1773. Jefferson was among the members who organized a committee to correspond with other colonies. In the spring of the following year, he was in the Virginia Assembly when

---

[4] Cooke, *Hamilton,* p. 6.
[5] James Thomas Flexner, *The Young Hamilton: A Biography* (Boston: Little, Brown, 1978), pp. 50–52, 454.

news reached Williamsburg of the dumping of tea into Boston Harbor, and he joined those who organized Virginia support for the New England protest.[6]

For both Thomas Jefferson and Alexander Hamilton, the American Revolution was a defining moment. The cataclysmal events of that upheaval set each man on a course that ultimately brought them together, as the young American nation took form. They experienced the Revolution from different circumstances and locations, but they shared a common commitment to the American cause for which they both risked their lives. There is, however, far less documentation about Hamilton's path to revolution than Jefferson's.

Hamilton did not stay long in New York after reaching America in 1773. He promptly went to Elizabethtown, New Jersey, and enrolled in a preparatory school conducted by Francis Barber, a recent Princeton graduate. Within a year, he overcame most of the deficiencies resulting from his lack of formal education, sufficiently mastering Latin, Greek, French, and mathematics to qualify for college admission. After failing to be admitted to Princeton, Hamilton enrolled in King's College in New York City, where he supplemented the inflexible curriculum with extensive reading in the college library. Although documents are limited in revealing Hamilton's reaction to the confrontation with Great Britain, he demonstrated his support of the American cause in pamphlets he wrote and had published in 1774 and 1775. He reaffirmed his commitment to the Revolution when he obtained a commission as a captain of an artillery company in the New York militia in March 1776.[7]

By this date, Jefferson had already gained wide recognition as a leading champion of the American cause. In May 1774, Lord Dunmore, the royal governor of Virginia, dissolved the House of Burgesses in response to rising support for the tea-dumping protest in Boston. During the summer, Jefferson — a member of the House of Burgesses before its dissolution — completed his *Summary View of the Rights of British America*. He prepared that paper for submission to a Virginia convention called to meet in Williamsburg in August. Jefferson's position was too extreme for the times — as he later admitted — and he confessed that his interpretation of the relationship of the colonies to Great Britain was one

[6] Cunningham, *In Pursuit of Reason,* pp. 14–16, 18, 21, 23–27.
[7] Cooke, *Hamilton,* pp. 7, 8, 12.

with which few of his colleagues agreed. But as a precursor to the Declaration of Independence, the writing is of particular interest.

The Virginia convention did not take up Jefferson's paper, but some members arranged to have it printed in Williamsburg. Publishers in Philadelphia and in London soon reprinted the twenty-three-page pamphlet. Although the author was identified only as "A Native and Member of the House of Burgesses," Jefferson's authorship became widely known.

After reviewing at length American grievances and claimed rights, Jefferson concluded with the following rousing summation.

THOMAS JEFFERSON

A Summary View of the Rights of British America

1774

. . . That these are our grievances which we have thus laid before his majesty, with that freedom of language and sentiment which becomes a free people claiming their rights, as derived from the laws of nature, and not as the gift of their chief magistrate: Let those flatter who fear, it is not an American art. To give praise which is not due might be well from the venal, but would ill beseem those who are asserting the rights of human nature. They know, and will therefore say, that kings are the servants, not the proprietors of the people. Open your breast, sire, to liberal and expanded thought. Let not the name of George the third be a blot in the page of history. You are surrounded by English counsellors, but remember that they are parties. You have no minister for American affairs, because you have none taken up from among us, nor amenable to the laws on which they are to give you advice. It behooves you, therefore, to think and to act for yourself and your people. The great principles of right and wrong are legible to every reader; to pursue them requires not the aid of many counsellors. The whole art of government consists in the art of being honest.

[Thomas Jefferson], *A Summary View of the Rights of British America, Set Forth in Some Resolutions Intended for the Inspection of the Present Delegates of the People of Virginia, Now in Convention.* By a Native and Member of the House of Burgesses (Williamsburg: Printed by Clementina Rind, [1774]). Reprinted from Paul L. Ford, ed., *The Works of Thomas Jefferson,* Federal Edition, 12 vols. (New York: G. P. Putnam's Sons, 1904), 2:86–89.

Only aim to do your duty, and mankind will give you credit where you fail. No longer persevere in sacrificing the rights of one part of the empire to the inordinate desires of another; but deal out to all equal and impartial right. Let no act be passed by any one legislature which may infringe on the rights and liberties of another. This is the important post in which fortune has placed you, holding the balance of a great, if a well poised empire. This, sire, is the advice of your great American council, on the observance of which may perhaps depend your felicity and future fame, and the preservation of that harmony which alone can continue both in Great Britain and America the reciprocal advantages of their connection. It is neither our wish nor our interest to separate from her. We are willing, on our part, to sacrifice everything which reason can ask to the restoration of that tranquillity for which all must wish. On their part, let them be ready to establish union and a generous plan. Let them name their terms, but let them be just. Accept of every commercial preference it is in our power to give for such things as we can raise for their use, or they make for ours. But let them not think to exclude us from going to other markets to dispose of those commodities which they cannot use, or to supply those wants which they cannot supply. Still less let it be proposed that our properties within our own territories shall be taxed or regulated by any power on earth but our own. The God who gave us life gave us liberty at the same time; the hand of force may destroy, but cannot disjoin them. This, sire, is our last, our determined resolution; and that you will be pleased to interpose with that efficacy which your earnest endeavors may ensure to procure redress of these our great grievances, to quiet the minds of your subjects in British America, against any apprehensions of future encroachment, to establish fraternal love and harmony through the whole empire, and that these may continue to the last ages of time, is the fervent prayer of all British America.

Hamilton also joined early on in the pamphlet skirmishes of the American Revolution. In December 1774, he published *A Full Vindication of the Measures of Congress,* followed in 1775 by a sequel, *The Farmer Refuted.*[8] In the latter pamphlet, Hamilton included a succinct summation of his views on the authority of the British Parliament over Americans.

---

[8] *The Farmer Refuted* was written in reply to Samuel Seabury's pamphlet *A View of the Controversy between Great Britain and Her Colonies* (New York, 1774), in Harold C. Syrett et al., eds., *The Papers of Alexander Hamilton,* 27 vols. (New York: Columbia University Press, 1961–87), 1:81.

ALEXANDER HAMILTON

The Farmer Refuted

February 23, 1775

. . . When I say, that the authority of parliament is confined to Great-Britain, I speak of it, in its primitive and original state. Parliament may acquire an incidental influence over others; but this must be by their own free consent. For without this, any power it might exercise, would be mere usurpation, and by no means a just authority.

The best way of determining disputes, and of investigating truth, is by descending to elementary principles. Any other method may only bewilder and misguide the understanding; but this will soon lead to a convincing and satisfactory crisis. By observing this method, we shall learn the following truths.

That the existence of the house of commons depends upon the people's right to a share in the legislature; which is exercised, by means of electing the members of that house. That the end and intention of this right is, to preserve the life, property and liberty of the subject, from the encroachments of oppression and tyranny.

That this end is accomplished, by means of the *intimate connexion* of interest, between those members and their constituents, the people of Great-Britain.

That with respect to the people of America, there is no such *intimate connexion* of interest; but the contrary. And therefore that end could not be answered to them; consequently the *end* ceasing, the *means* must cease also.

That the house of commons derives all its power, from its own real constituents, who are the people of Great-Britain, and that therefore, it has no power, but what they *originally* had in themselves.

That they had no original right to the life, property, or liberty of Americans; nor any acquired from their own consent, and of course could give no authority over them.

That, therefore, the house of commons has no such authority.

What need is there of a multiplicity of arguments, or a long chain of reasoning to inculcate these luminous principles? They speak the plainest language to every man of common sense; and must carry conviction where the mental eye is not bedimmed, by the mist of prejudice, partiality, ambition, or avarice. . . .

Harold C. Syrett et al., eds., *The Papers of Alexander Hamilton,* 27 vols. (New York: Columbia University Press, 1961–87), 1:96–97.

Thomas Jefferson was far more directly involved in the early events of the American Revolution than was Alexander Hamilton. Although Jefferson was not one of Virginia's delegates to the first Continental Congress, which met in Philadelphia in September 1774, his *Summary View of the Rights of British America* circulated among the delegates. Jefferson was present at the second Virginia convention that met in Richmond in March 1775, having been elected as one of two delegates from Albemarle County. He left little record of that dramatic convention, which was dominated by Patrick Henry, but Jefferson fully supported Henry's proposal to arm and train a militia to defend Virginia. The Richmond convention also named Jefferson to succeed Peyton Randolph in the Continental Congress should Randolph be unable to serve, which turned out to be the case.[9]

Virginia's Governor Dunmore issued a proclamation on March 28 denouncing the Continental Congress. On the night of April 20, he secretly had gunpowder moved from the Williamsburg Magazine to a British warship in the York River. Before the end of the month, the news of the bloodshed on April 19 between British troops and minutemen at Lexington and Concord reached Virginia. After attending the Virginia House of Burgesses for ten days, Jefferson set out for Philadelphia on June 11 to attend the Continental Congress. He carried with him a copy of the resolutions that the burgesses had prepared to present to the Virginia governor, Lord Dunmore, rejecting the conciliatory proposals of British minister Lord North. While Jefferson was en route to Philadelphia, the Continental Congress named George Washington the commander in chief of all continental forces. When Washington departed for Boston to take charge of the army on June 23, two days after Jefferson's arrival in Philadelphia, Jefferson wrote privately, "The war is now heartily entered into, without a prospect of accommodation but thro' the effectual interposition of arms."[10]

Jefferson's reputation as a writer had preceded him, especially through his *Summary View of the Rights of British America*. He was soon playing a leading role in drafting the major papers issued by the Congress, including the "Declaration of the Causes and Necessity of Taking

[9]Cunningham, *In Pursuit of Reason,* pp. 31–33.
[10]Jefferson to Francis Eppes, June 26, 1775, in Julian P. Boyd, Charles T. Cullen, and John Catanzariti, eds., *The Papers of Thomas Jefferson,* 27 vols. to date (Princeton: Princeton University Press, 1950–), 1:174; Cunningham, *In Pursuit of Reason,* pp. 33–36.

up Arms" and the response to Lord North's conciliatory plan. Within six weeks of his arrival, Jefferson was among the leading men in the Congress. His major fame came a year later when the Congress named him to the committee to draft a declaration of independence. Although John Adams and Benjamin Franklin, as members of the drafting committee, made suggestions and changes that Jefferson incorporated into the declaration and the Congress made additional alterations before its adoption, Jefferson was the principal author. He claimed no originality for the principles enunciated in the Declaration of Independence, but the philosophy of natural rights on which the declaration was based was fundamental to his own beliefs.[11]

The contradiction of a slaveholder declaring that all men are created equal is glaring today. In Jefferson's mind, however, slavery was contrary to natural law and existed only because of unenlightened monarchs or wicked legislatures. Once slavery was abolished, as he thought it must be, slaves would regain their natural status as free people. His original draft of the Declaration of Independence had contained a statement denouncing George III for disallowing colonial laws passed to suppress the slave trade. Jefferson had written,

> He has waged cruel war against human nature itself, violating it's most sacred rights of life and liberty in the persons of a distant people who never offended him, captivating and carrying them into slavery in another hemisphere, or to incur miserable death in their transportation thither. This piratical warfare, the opprobrium of *infidel* powers, is the warfare of the CHRISTIAN king of Great Britain. Determined to keep open a market where MEN should be bought and sold, he has prostituted his negative for suppressing every legislative attempt to prohibit or to restrain this execrable commerce; and that this assemblage of horrors might want no fact of distinguished die, he is now exciting those very people to rise in arms among us, and to purchase that liberty of which *he* has deprived them, by murdering the people upon whom *he* also obtruded them; thus paying off former crimes committed against the *liberties* of one people, with crimes which he urges them to commit against the *lives* of another.[12]

Along with other changes, Congress struck out this passage. Whereas Virginia members supported Jefferson's condemnation of slavery, South Carolinians and Georgians opposed it in the Congress, and some northern members were dubious about the sweeping condemnation of a

[11] Cunningham, *In Pursuit of Reason,* pp. 36–39, 41–43, 46–51.

[12] Jefferson's "original Rough draught" of the Declaration of Independence, in Boyd, Cullen, and Catanzariti, eds., *Jefferson Papers,* 1:426.

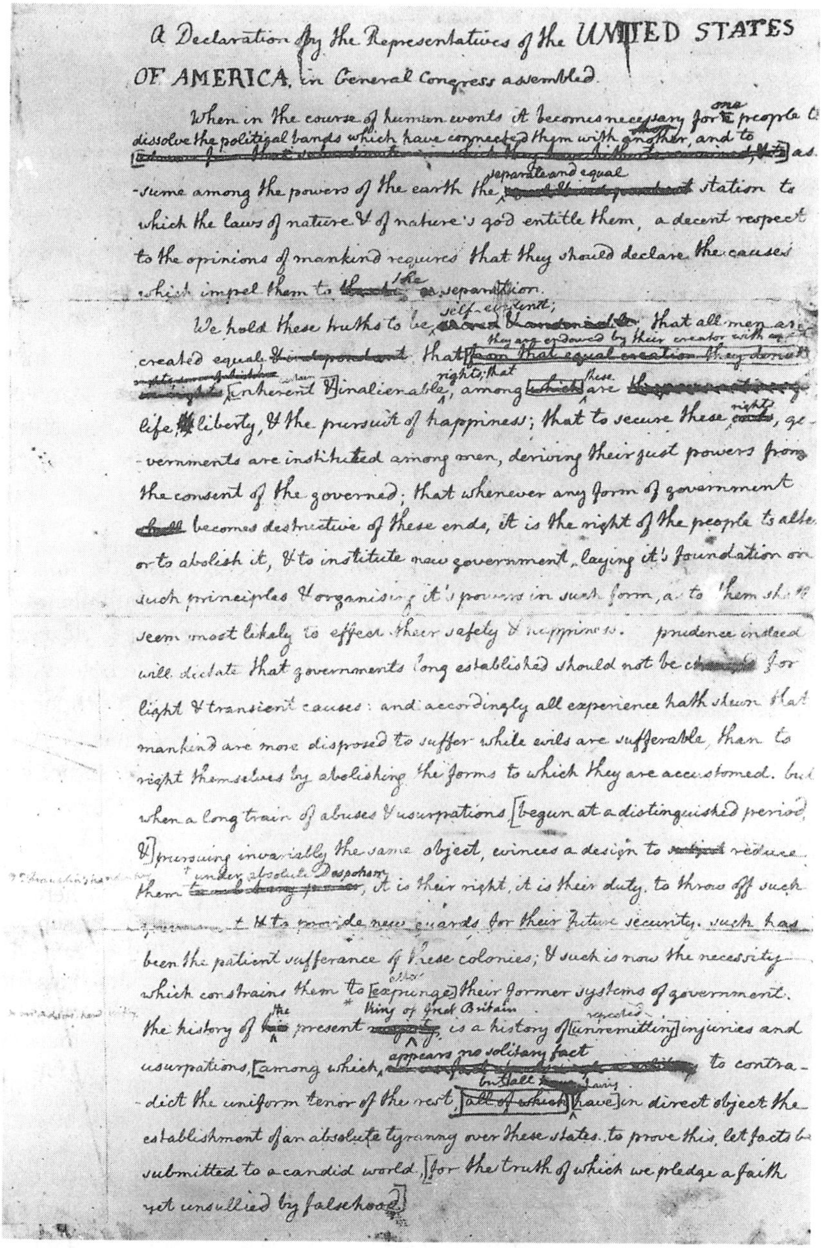
A Declaration by the Representatives of the UNITED STATES OF AMERICA, in General Congress assembled.

When in the course of human events it becomes necessary for one people to dissolve the political bands which have connected them with another, and to assume among the powers of the earth the separate and equal station to which the laws of nature & of nature's god entitle them, a decent respect to the opinions of mankind requires that they should declare the causes which impel them to the separation.

We hold these truths to be self-evident; that all men are created equal; that they are endowed by their creator with inherent & inalienable rights; that among these are life, liberty, & the pursuit of happiness; that to secure these rights, governments are instituted among men, deriving their just powers from the consent of the governed; that whenever any form of government becomes destructive of these ends, it is the right of the people to alter or to abolish it, & to institute new government, laying it's foundation on such principles & organising it's powers in such form, as to them shall seem most likely to effect their safety & happiness. prudence indeed will dictate that governments long established should not be changed for light & transient causes: and accordingly all experience hath shewn that mankind are more disposed to suffer while evils are sufferable, than to right themselves by abolishing the forms to which they are accustomed. but when a long train of abuses & usurpations [begun at a distinguished period, &] pursuing invariably the same object, evinces a design to reduce them under absolute Despotism, it is their right, it is their duty, to throw off such government, & to provide new guards for their future security. such has been the patient sufferance of these colonies; & such is now the necessity which constrains them to [expunge] their former systems of government. the history of the present king of Great Britain is a history of [unremitting] injuries and usurpations, [among which, appears no solitary fact to contradict the uniform tenor of the rest, but all have] in direct object the establishment of an absolute tyranny over these states. to prove this, let facts be submitted to a candid world, [for the truth of which we pledge a faith yet unsullied by falsehood]

Figure 1. *Page of Thomas Jefferson's Original Draft of the Declaration of Independence.*
Manuscript Division, Library of Congress.

slave trade in which northern shipowners had been engaged.[13] Jefferson in general questioned most of the changes made in his draft, though some of them did strengthen the document. The absence of a condemnation of slavery in the Declaration of Independence, however, was a dangerous harbinger for the future of the emerging new nation. Hamilton was apparently indifferent to slavery in his early years, but whereas Jefferson in later years moderated his opposition to slavery, Hamilton moved in the opposite direction.

After the adoption of the Declaration of Independence, Jefferson anxiously returned to Virginia, for it was in the states where new governments were to be created. Although he forwarded his plan of a constitution for Virginia to Williamsburg, it arrived after most of the new state constitution had been drafted. It would be October 1776 before Jefferson could reclaim his seat in the Virginia House of Delegates.

For much of the next three years, Jefferson directed his attention to revising the laws of Virginia. Some of his reforms, including abolishing entail (which limited property inheritance to the owner's lineal descendants) and primogeniture (the exclusive right of inheritance belonging to the eldest son), would be adopted. Others, such as his proposed statute for religious freedom, would take several years to be enacted, and his plan for public education never was enacted as proposed. Although Jefferson favored the gradual emancipation of slaves, it never happened in Jefferson's Virginia.[14]

In June 1779, the House of Delegates elected Jefferson governor of Virginia to succeed Patrick Henry, who had served the three one-year terms permitted by the Virginia Constitution. Reelected in 1780, Jefferson declined to accept a third term in June 1781. During the difficult years of his governorship, when the British brought the war directly into Virginia, Jefferson and Hamilton had their first indirect contact.

By this time, Hamilton was an aide to General Washington. Hamilton had seen some military action in 1776 and 1777 in New York, and he was with Washington's forces in engagements at New Brunswick, Trenton, and Princeton. Although there is no record of any particular circumstance that might have attracted Washington's attention, someone recommended the young captain to the general, who on March 1, 1777,

---

[13]Dumas Malone, *Jefferson and His Time,* 6 vols. (Boston: Little, Brown, 1948–81), 1:222.

[14]Cunningham, *In Pursuit of Reason,* pp. 52–63.

added Hamilton to his staff as an aide-de-camp, with the rank of lieutenant colonel. One of thirty-two aides, Hamilton was not Washington's closest assistant, but he was in the inner circle of the high command.[15] His major task was letter writing, and in this capacity he drafted several letters from General Washington to Governor Jefferson.[16]

Hamilton also carried out special missions for General Washington. While on one assignment, Hamilton met Elizabeth Schuyler, the daughter of General Philip Schuyler, the head of a wealthy New York landed family and an early and strong supporter of the Revolution. In March 1780, Hamilton and Elizabeth Schuyler became engaged, and they were married at the Schuyler mansion in Albany on December 14, 1780. Elizabeth returned with Hamilton to General Washington's headquarters at Windsor, New York.[17]

In April 1781, Hamilton resigned from Washington's staff, and in July of that year he was given command of a battalion of light infantry. With Washington's army as it moved south to Virginia in late August, Hamilton saw major action at the battle of Yorktown. On October 14, he led the assault and capture of Redoubt No. 10 (an enclosed British defensive position) in that triumphal American victory.

Neither Thomas Jefferson nor Alexander Hamilton left any account, known today, of their first meeting. Among the voluminous papers of both men, no clear evidence has been found to indicate when their paths first crossed. The two men must have known of one another before they met in person. Through his opposition to British colonial policy, Jefferson's reputation spread beyond Virginia. The younger man's name may have become known to Jefferson after Hamilton joined General Washington's staff in 1777. But Jefferson left the governorship before Washington's army moved south from New York for the campaign that would defeat Cornwallis's army at Yorktown. No record has been found of Jefferson's and Hamilton's meeting during the Revolution.

It is probable, even likely, that Hamilton and Jefferson met in Philadelphia in late 1782 or early 1783 while Hamilton was a member of the Continental Congress. Jefferson arrived in Philadelphia on December 27, 1782, having been appointed to join the peace commission in Paris, and

---

[15] Cooke, *Hamilton,* pp. 13–15.

[16] Washington to Jefferson, Dec. 11, 1779, Feb. 6, 1781, in Syrett et al., eds., *Hamilton Papers,* 2:225, 553.

[17] Broadus Mitchell, *Alexander Hamilton: The National Adventure, 1788–1804* (New York: Macmillan, 1962), pp. 196–97.

he spent a month in Philadelphia studying documents in the Department of Foreign Affairs in preparation for a mission that he would never make. James Madison was then a member of Congress, and Jefferson roomed at Mrs. Mary House's boardinghouse, where Madison lived. As a member of Congress from New York, Hamilton served on committees with Madison while Jefferson was in Philadelphia.[18] It would be surprising if Jefferson and Hamilton did not meet at this time.

The following year, when Jefferson took a seat in the Continental Congress in November 1783, Hamilton was no longer a member. After being appointed as minister plenipotentiary to negotiate treaties of amity and commerce in Europe, Jefferson spent a week in New York in 1784 before sailing from Boston in early July for France, but there is no record of his having any contact with Hamilton. Succeeding Benjamin Franklin as American minister to France in 1785, Jefferson would not return to the United States until October 1789.

Jefferson was in France when the Constitutional Convention met in Philadelphia during the spring and summer of 1787. On the other hand, Hamilton was a delegate from New York to the convention, and he had been a leading voice at the Annapolis Convention in September 1786, which called for the Constitutional Convention to meet. From Paris, Jefferson had not shared the alarm of many in reacting to the rebellion in Massachusetts of destitute farmers led by Daniel Shays, who had been a captain during the Revolutionary War. Hamilton condemned Shays's actions and called for suppressing the uprising by force, but Jefferson wrote privately, "God forbid we should ever be 20 years without such a rebellion. . . . What country can preserve it's [*sic*] liberties if their rulers are not warned from time to time that their people preserve the spirit of resistance? . . . The tree of liberty must be refreshed from time to time with the blood of patriots and tyrants." [19]

At the Constitutional Convention in Philadelphia, Hamilton took the floor on June 18, 1787, to express his dissatisfaction with both the Virginia and the New Jersey Plans that had been placed before the assem-

---

[18] William T. Hutchinson et al., eds., *The Papers of James Madison,* 17 vols. (Chicago and Charlottesville: University Press of Virginia, 1962–91), 5:466–69, 473, 6:64; Malone, *Jefferson,* 1:400; Syrett et al., eds., *Hamilton Papers,* 3:229–30, 233–34; Boyd, Cullen, and Catanzariti, eds., *Jefferson Papers,* 6:217n, 7:2.

[19] Jefferson to William Stephens Smith, Nov. 13, 1787, in Boyd, Cullen, and Catanzariti, eds., *Jefferson Papers,* 12:356.

blage. The Virginia Plan, which proposed abandoning the Articles of Confederation and creating a new national government, called for a bicameral national legislature, an executive chosen by the legislature, a judiciary that included a supreme court and inferior courts, and a council of revision with a veto over legislative acts. The opposing New Jersey Plan stressed retention of the Articles of Confederation with increased powers given to Congress to tax, regulate commerce, and choose a plural executive and members of a supreme court.

Behind closed doors, Hamilton proposed a more powerful central government than that envisioned by the Virginia Plan. In the course of a long speech, he candidly expressed his doubts about the capacity of people for self-government. The notes taken by four members while Hamilton was speaking — not made public under the rules of the convention — today provide summaries of Hamilton's lengthy address. The following excerpts are extracted from the two most detailed accounts by James Madison of Virginia and Robert Yates, a colleague of Hamilton's from New York.

JAMES MADISON

Summary of Hamilton's Response to the New Jersey and Virginia Plans

June 18, 1787

Mr. Hamilton, had been hitherto silent on the business before the Convention, partly from respect to others whose superior abilities age & experience rendered him unwilling to bring forward ideas dissimilar to theirs, and partly from his delicate situation with respect to his own State, to whose sentiments as expressed by his Colleagues, he could by no means accede. The crisis however which now marked our affairs, was too serious to permit any scruples whatever to prevail over the duty imposed on every man to contribute his efforts for the public safety & happiness. He was obliged therefore to declare himself unfriendly to both plans. He was particularly opposed to that from N. Jersey, being fully convinced, that

Harold C. Syrett et al., eds., *The Papers of Alexander Hamilton,* 27 vols. (New York: Columbia University Press, 1961–87), 4:187–93.

no amendment of the Confederation, leaving the States in possession of their Sovereignty could possibly answer the purpose. On the other hand he confessed he was much discouraged by the amazing extent of Country in expecting the desired blessings from any general sovereignty that could be substituted. . . .

The great question is what provision shall we make for the happiness of our Country? He would first make a comparative examination of the two plans — prove that there were essential defects in both — and point out such changes as might render a *national one,* efficacious. The great & essential principles necessary for the support of Government are 1. an active & constant interest in supporting it. This principle does not exist in the States in favor of the federal Govt. They have evidently in a high degree, the esprit de corps. They constantly pursue internal interests adverse to those of the whole. They have their particular debts — their particular plans of finance &c. All these when opposed to, invariably prevail over the requisitions & plans of Congress. 2. The love of power. Men love power. The same remarks are applicable to this principle. The States have constantly shewn a disposition rather to regain the powers delegated by them than to part with more, or to give effect to what they had parted with. The ambition of their demagogues is known to hate the controul of the Genl. Government. It may be remarked too that the Citizens have not that anxiety to prevent a dissolution of the Genl. Govt. as of the particular Govts. A dissolution of the latter would be fatal; of the former would still leave the purposes of Govt. attainable to a considerable degree. Consider what such a State as Virga. will be in a few years, a few compared with the life of nations. How strongly will it feel its importance & self-sufficiency? 3. An habitual attachment of the people. The whole force of this tie is on the side of the State Govt. Its sovereignty is immediately before the eyes of the people: its protection is immediately enjoyed by them. From its hand distributive justice, and all those acts which familiarize & endear Govt. to a people, are dispensed to them. 4. *Force* by which may be understood a *coertion of laws* or *coertion of arms.* Congs. have not the former except in few cases. In particular States, this coercion is nearly sufficient; tho' he held it in most cases, not entirely so. A certain portion of military force is absolutely necessary in large communities. Masss. is now feeling this necessity & making provision for it. But how can this force be exerted on the States collectively. It is impossible. It amounts to a war between the parties. Foreign powers also will not be idle spectators. They will interpose, the confusion will increase, and a dissolution of the Union will ensue. 5. *influence.* he did not mean corruption, but a dispensation of those regular honors & emoluments, which produce an attachment to the Govt. Almost all the weight of these is on the side of the States; and must continue so as long as the States continue to exist. All the passions then we see, of avarice, ambition, interest, which govern most individuals, and all public bodies, fall into the current of the States, and do not flow in the stream of the Genl. Govt. The former therefore will generally be an over-match for the Genl. Govt. and render any confederacy, in its very nature precarious. . . .

ROBERT YATES

Summary of Hamilton's Response to the New Jersey and Virginia Plans

June 18, 1787

Mr. Hamilton. To deliver my sentiments on so important a subject, when the first characters in the union have gone before me, inspires me with the greatest diffidence, especially when my own ideas are so materially dissimilar to the plans now before the committee. My situation is disagreeable, but it would be criminal not to come forward on a question of such magnitude. I have well considered the subject, and am convinced that no amendment of the confederation can answer the purpose of a good government, so long as state sovereignties do, in any shape, exist; and I have great doubts whether a national government on the Virginia plan can be made effectual. . . .

    Let us take a review of the variety of important objects, which must necessarily engage the attention of a national government. You have to protect your rights against Canada on the north, Spain on the south, and your western frontier against the savages. You have to adopt necessary plans for the settlement of your frontiers, and to institute the mode in which settlements and good government are to be made.

    How is the expense of supporting and regulating these important matters to be defrayed? By requisition on the states, according to the Jersey plan? Will this do it? We have already found it ineffectual. Let one state prove delinquent, and it will encourage others to follow the example; and thus the whole will fail. And what is the standard to quota among the states their respective proportions? Can lands be the standard? How would that apply between Russia and Holland? Compare Pennsylvania with North-Carolina, or Connecticut with New-York. Does not commerce or industry in the one or other make a great disparity between these different countries, and may not the comparative value of the states from these circumstances, make an unequal disproportion when the data is numbers? I

Harold C. Syrett et al., eds., *The Papers of Alexander Hamilton,* 27 vols. (New York: Columbia University Press, 1961–87), 4:195–201.

therefore conclude that either system would ultimately destroy the confederation, or any other government which is established on such fallacious principles. Perhaps imposts, taxes on specific articles, would produce a more equal system of drawing a revenue.

Another objection against the Jersey plan is, the unequal representation. Can the great States consent to this? If they did it would eventually work its own destruction. How are forces to be raised by the Jersey plan? By quotas? Will the states comply with the requisition? As much as they will with the taxes.

Examine the present confederation, and it is evident they can raise no troops nor equip vessels before war is actually declared. They cannot therefore take any preparatory measure before an enemy is at your door. How unwise and inadequate their powers! and this must ever be the case when you attempt to define powers. Something will always be wanting. Congress, by being annually elected, and subject to recall, will ever come with the prejudices of their states rather than the good of the union. Add therefore additional powers to a body thus organized, and you establish a *sovereignty* of the worst kind, consisting of a single body. Where are the checks? None. They must either prevail over the state governments, or the prevalence of the state governments must end in their dissolution. This is a conclusive objection to the Jersey plan.

Such are the insuperable objections to both plans: and what is to be done on this occasion? I confess I am at a loss. I foresee the difficulty on a consolidated plan of drawing a representation from so extensive a continent to one place. What can be the inducements for gentlemen to come 600 miles to a national legislature? The expense would at least amount to £100,000. This however can be no conclusive objection if it eventuates in an extinction of state governments. The burthen of the latter would be saved, and the expense then would not be great. State distinctions would be found unnecessary, and yet I confess, to carry government to the extremities, the state governments reduced to corporations, and with very limited powers, might be necessary, and the expense of the national government become less burthensome.

Yet, I confess, I see great difficulty of drawing forth a good representation. What, for example, will be the inducements for gentlemen of fortune and abilities to leave their houses and business to attend annually and long? It cannot be the wages; for these, I presume, must be small. Will not the power, therefore, be thrown into the hands of the demagogue or middling politician, who, for the sake of a small stipend and the hopes of advancement, will offer himself as a candidate, and the real men of weight and influence, by remaining at home, add strength to the state governments? I am at a loss to know what must be done; I despair that a republican form of government can remove the difficulties. Whatever may be my opinion, I would hold it however unwise to change that form of government. I believe the British government forms the best model the world ever produced, and such has been its progress in the minds of the many, that this truth gradually gains ground. This government has for its object *public strength* and *individual security*. It is said with us to be unattainable. If it was once formed it would maintain itself. All communities divide themselves into the few and the many. The first are the rich and well born, the other the mass of the people. The voice of the people has been said to be the voice of God; and however generally this maxim has been quoted and believed, it is not true in fact. The people are turbulent and changing; they seldom judge or determine right. Give therefore to the first class a distinct, permanent share in the government. They will check the unsteadiness of the second, and as they cannot receive any advantage by a change, they therefore will ever maintain good government. Can a democratic assembly, who annually revolve in the mass of the people, be supposed steadily to pursue the public good? Nothing but a permanent body can check the imprudence of democracy. Their turbulent and uncontrouling disposition requires checks. The senate of New-York, although chosen for four years, we have found to be inefficient. Will, on the Virginia plan, a continuance of seven years do it? It is admitted, that you cannot have a good executive upon a democratic plan. See the excellency of the British executive. He is placed above temptation. He can have no distinct interests from the public welfare. Nothing short of such an executive can be efficient. The weak side of a republican government is the danger of foreign influence. This is unavoidable, unless it is so constructed as to bring forward its first characters in its support. I am therefore for a general government, yet would wish to go the full length of republican principles.

Let one body of the legislature be constituted during good behaviour or life.

Let one executive be appointed who dares execute his powers.

It may be asked is this a republican system? It is strictly so, as long as they remain elective.

And let me observe, that an executive is less dangerous to the liberties of the people when in office during life, than for seven years. . . .

Fifty years later, after reading the notes that James Madison had taken at the Constitutional Convention, John Quincy Adams, a former president and then a member of the House of Representatives, recorded in his diary:

> I read this morning in the manuscripts of Mr. Madison the report of the speech of Alexander Hamilton in the Convention of 1787, upon presenting *his* plan for a Constitution of the United States. The speech occupied a whole day, and was of great ability. The plan was theoretically better than

that which was adopted, but energetic, and approaching the British Constitution far closer, and such as the public opinions of that day never would have tolerated. Still less would it be endured by the democratic spirit of the present age — far more democratic than that; for, after half a century of inextinguishable wars between the democracy of the European race and its monarchy and aristocracy, the democracy is yet in the ascendant, and gaining victory after victory over the porcelain of the race. If Hamilton were now living, he would not dare, in an assembly of Americans, even with closed doors, to avow the opinions of this speech, or to present such a plan even as a speculation.[20]

Although Hamilton would have gone farther in creating a dominant national government than did the Philadelphia convention, he supported the final instrument drafted by the convention and became one of its leading champions during the ratification process. Joined by James Madison and John Jay, Hamilton contributed the greatest number of essays for the *Federalist* papers, the most important and influential commentary on the Constitution at the time of its ratification.

With the members of the Constitutional Convention sworn to secrecy, Jefferson remained in the dark about the proceedings until November 1787, when he received his first copy of the proposed constitution from John Adams in London. In December, Jefferson finally received a long letter that Madison had written to him in September reporting on the proceedings. In his reply to Madison on December 20, 1787, Jefferson expressed approval of the separation of powers among the legislative, executive, and judicial branches. He liked the requirements that the House of Representatives initiate tax legislation and that voting in Congress be by individual members, not by states. Among his objections, Jefferson expressed disappointment that no bill of rights was included in the proposed constitution and that the president would be eligible for re-election.

[20] Charles Francis Adams, ed., *The Memoirs of John Quincy Adams, Comprising Portions of His Diary from 1797 to 1848,* 12 vols. (Philadelphia: J. B. Lippincott, 1874–77), Apr. 8, 1837, 9:345.

THOMAS JEFFERSON

Letter to James Madison

December 20, 1787

The season admitting only of operations in the Cabinet, and these being in a great measure secret, I have little to fill a letter. I will therefore make up the deficiency by adding a few words on the Constitution proposed by our Convention. I like much the general idea of framing a government which should go on of itself peaceably, without needing continual recurrence to the state legislatures. I like the organization of the government into Legislative, Judiciary and Executive. I like the power given the Legislature to levy taxes; and for that reason solely approve of the greater house being chosen by the people directly. For tho' I think a house chosen by them will be very illy qualified to legislate for the Union, for foreign nations etc. yet this evil does not weigh against the good of preserving inviolate the fundamental principle that the people are not to be taxed but by representatives chosen immediately by themselves. I am captivated by the compromise of the opposite claims of the great and little states, of the latter to equal, and the former to proportional influence. I am much pleased too with the substitution of the method of voting by persons, instead of that of voting by states: and I like the negative given to the Executive with a third of either house, though I should have liked it better had the Judiciary been associated for that purpose, or invested with a similar and separate power. There are other good things of less moment. I will now add what I do not like. First the omission of a bill of rights providing clearly and without the aid of sophisms for freedom of religion, freedom of the press, protection against standing armies, restriction against monopolies, the eternal and unremitting force of the habeas corpus laws, and trials by jury in all matters of fact triable by the laws of the land and not by the law of Nations. . . . Let me add that a bill of rights is what the people are entitled to against every government on earth, general or particular, and what no just government should refuse, or rest on inference. The second feature I dislike, and greatly dislike, is the abandonment in every instance of the necessity of rotation in office, and most particularly in the case of the President. Experience concurs with reason in concluding that the first magistrate will always be re-elected if the constitution permits it. He is then an officer for life. This once observed it becomes of so much consequence to certain nations to have a friend or a foe at the head of our affairs that they will interfere with money and with arms. . . . The election of a

James Morton Smith, ed., *The Republic of Letters: The Correspondence between Thomas Jefferson and James Madison, 1776–1826,* 3 vols. (New York: W. W. Norton, 1995), 1:512–14.

President of America some years hence will be much more interesting to certain nations of Europe than ever the election of a king of Poland was. Reflect on all the instances in history antient and modern, of elective monarchies, and say if they do not give foundation for my fears, the Roman emperors, the popes, while they were of any importance, the German emperors till they became hereditary in practice, the kings of Poland, the Deys of the Ottoman dependancies. It may be said that if elections are to be attended with these disorders, the seldomer they are renewed the better. But experience shews that the only way to prevent disorder is to render them uninteresting by frequent changes. An incapacity to be elected a second time would have been the only effectual preventative. The power of removing him every fourth year by the vote of the people is a power which will not be exercised. The king of Poland is removeable every day by the Diet, yet he is never removed.

Smaller objections are the Appeal in fact as well as law, and the binding all persons Legislative, Executive and Judiciary by oath to maintain that constitution. I do not pretend to decide what would be the best method of procuring the establishment of the manifold good things in this constitution, and of getting rid of the bad. Whether by adopting it in hopes of future amendment, or, after it has been duly weighed and canvassed by the people, after seeing the parts they generally dislike, and those they generally approve, to say to them 'We see now what you wish. Send together your deputies again, let them frame a constitution for you omitting what you have condemned, and establishing the powers you approve. Even these will be a great addition to the energy of your government.'

At all events I hope you will not be discouraged from other trials, if the present one should fail of it's full effect.

I have thus told you freely what I like and dislike: merely as a matter of curiosity for I know your own judgment has been formed on all these points after having heard every thing which could be urged on them. I own I am not a friend to a very energetic government. It is always oppressive. The late [Shays's] rebellion in Massachusets has given more alarm than I think it should have done. Calculate that one rebellion in 13 states in the course of 11 years, is but one for each state in a century and a half. No country should be so long without one. Nor will any degree of power in the hands of government prevent insurrections. France with all its' despotism, and two or three hundred thousand men always in arms has had three insurrections in the three years I have been here in every one of which greater numbers were engaged than in Massachusets and a great deal more blood was spilt. In Turkey, which Montesquieu supposes more despotic, insurrections are the events of every day. In England, where the hand of power is lighter than here, but heavier than with us they happen every half dozen years. Compare again the ferocious depredations of their insurgents with the order, the moderation and the almost self extinguishment of ours.

After all, it is my principle that the will of the Majority should always prevail. If they approve the proposed Convention in all it's parts, I shall concur in it chearfully, in hopes that they will amend it whenever they shall find it work wrong. I think our governments will remain virtuous for many centuries; as long as they are chiefly agricultural; and this will be as long as there shall be vacant lands in any part of America. When they get piled upon one another in large cities, as in Europe, they will become corrupt as in Europe. Above all things I hope the education of the common people will be attended to; convinced that on their good sense we may rely with the most security for the preservation of a due degree of liberty.

After detailing the constitutional features that he liked and disliked, Jefferson closed by indicating his willingness to accept the new instrument as drafted. To another correspondent Jefferson wrote that, were he in America, he would advocate the Constitution warmly until nine states ratified it and then urge the remaining states to withhold their approval until a declaration of rights was added.[21] When word of this view circulated in the United States, it caused some embarrassment to champions of the Constitution, but meanwhile Jefferson changed his mind and supported following the model of Massachusetts in ratifying the Constitution and proposing amendments at the same time.[22]

Jefferson remained in France as the American minister while ratification was being debated and voted upon in the state conventions. He did not return to America until after the new Constitution went into effect. Meanwhile, events in France even more momentous than those in the United States riveted Jefferson's attention. He was present in Versailles when the Estates General met on May 4, 1789 — only a few days after Washington had been inaugurated as president in New York on April 30. The American minister followed with high interest the unfolding events of the French Revolution as the National Assembly was proclaimed and King Louis XVI allowed it to proceed. Jefferson was in Paris on July 14, when the Bastille was stormed. The Marquis de Lafayette — who had aided Americans during their revolt against Great Britain — and others consulted Jefferson as they drafted the French Declaration of

[21] Jefferson to William Stephens Smith, Feb. 2, 1788, in Boyd, Cullen, and Catanzariti, eds., *Jefferson Papers*, 12:558.
[22] Cunningham, *In Pursuit of Reason*, pp. 117–18.

the Rights of Man. Jefferson himself recognized that he had witnessed "such events as will be for ever memorable in history," noting his singular fortune "to see in the course of fourteen years two such revolutions as were never before seen."[23] The scenes that he witnessed in France would later shape Jefferson's sympathy for the French revolutionary cause.

Jefferson left Paris in September 1789 to return to the United States on his first leave since arriving in France in 1784. When he arrived in Virginia in November, he found a country greatly changed since his departure. A new constitution had been adopted, a new congress assembled, and the first president elected and inaugurated. Jefferson also learned for the first time that President Washington had named him as the secretary of state and that the Senate had already confirmed the appointment. Expecting to return to Paris to watch the unfolding of events there, Jefferson was reluctant to assume the new post, which in addition to the conduct of foreign affairs was charged with oversight of all domestic concerns not administered by the Treasury Department. But yielding to the wishes of the president and the advice of Madison, Jefferson accepted the appointment as the first secretary of state.

In March 1790, when Jefferson arrived in New York — the temporary capital — to assume his duties, Hamilton had been at his post as secretary of the Treasury since September 1789. Hamilton's appointment had come not because he had been an aide to General Washington during the Revolutionary War, but because of his knowledge of financial affairs in an age when few men in the United States were experienced in financial matters.

The difference in the fundamental political outlooks of Jefferson and Hamilton as they joined Washington's cabinet may be most strikingly seen by comparing Hamilton's speech at the Constitutional Convention of 1787 quoted above (pages 15–19) with the brief remarks that Jefferson addressed to his neighbors in Albemarle County, Virginia, in February 1790 before leaving for New York. In replying to the address of his neighbors welcoming him home upon his return from France, Jefferson compressed into a brief response an affirmation of his firm belief in reason, natural law, and the rights of man; and he affirmed his faith in majority rule.

---

[23] Jefferson to Madison, July 22, 1789, Jefferson to Maria Cosway, July 25, 1789, in Boyd, Cullen, and Catanzariti, eds., *Jefferson Papers,* 15:299, 305; Cunningham, *In Pursuit of Reason,* pp. 123–26.

THOMAS JEFFERSON

Address to His Neighbors

February 12, 1790

Gentlemen:

The testimony of esteem with which you are pleased to honour my return to my native county fills me with gratitude and pleasure. While it shews that my absence has not lost me your friendly recollection, it holds out the comfortable hope that when the hour of retirement shall come, I shall again find myself amidst those with whom I have long lived, with whom I wish to live, and whose affection is the source of my purest happiness. Their favor was the door thro' which I was ushered on the stage of public life; and while I have been led on thro' it's varying scenes, I could not be unmindful of those who assigned me my first part.

My feeble and obscure exertions in their service, and in the holy cause of freedom, have had no other merit than that they were my best. We have all the same. We have been fellow-labourers and fellow-sufferers, and heaven has rewarded us with a happy issue from our struggles. It rests now with ourselves alone to enjoy in peace and concord the blessings of self-government, so long denied to mankind: to shew by example the sufficiency of human reason for the care of human affairs and that the will of the majority, the Natural law of every society, is the only sure guardian of the rights of man. Perhaps even this may sometimes err. But it's errors are honest, solitary and short-lived.— Let us then, my dear friends, for ever bow down to the general reason of the society. We are safe with that, even in it's deviations, for it soon returns again to the right way. These are lessons we have learnt together. We have prospered in their practice, and the liberality with which you are pleased to approve my attachment to the general rights of mankind assures me we are still together in these it's kindred sentiments.

Wherever I may be stationed, by the will of my country, it will be my delight to see, in the general tide of happiness, that yours too flows on in just place and measure. That it may flow thro' all times, gathering strength as it goes, and spreading the happy influence of reason and liberty over the face of the earth, is my fervent prayer to heaven.

FEB. 12. 1790.

Julian P. Boyd, Charles T. Cullen, and John Catanzariti, eds., *The Papers of Thomas Jefferson,* 27 vols. to date (Princeton: Princeton University Press, 1950–), 16:178–79.

Figure 2. *Thomas Jefferson.*
Oil portrait painted from life by Charles Willson Peale, circa 1791.
Independence National Historical Park Collection, Philadelphia.

2
Diverging Courses

In creating the executive departments, Congress — guarding its power to tax and appropriate money — required the secretary of the Treasury to report directly to the legislature, while other department heads reported through the president. On September 21, 1789, soon after the Senate confirmed Alexander Hamilton's appointment as secretary of the Treasury, the House of Representatives directed him to prepare a report on the public credit. Because of the large debt incurred during the Revolutionary War, this was one of the most pressing issues facing the new government.

After discussions in the House as to whether the secretary of the Treasury should report in person or in writing, the House set the precedent of having such reports submitted in writing. Applying himself to the task with customary diligence and dispatch, Hamilton compiled a detailed report on public finances. He submitted his *Report on the Public Credit* to the House of Representatives on January 14, 1790 — a month before Thomas Jefferson accepted appointment as secretary of state. After ordering three hundred copies of the report printed, the House began debate on Hamilton's proposals on February 8. When Jefferson arrived in New York on March 21 to take up his duties as secretary of state, Hamilton's report was the dominant public issue before Congress and the country.

The initial printed text of Hamilton's *Report on the Public Credit* filled fifty-one folio pages, including nine schedules and a text of the proposed act. Behind the bland title of the report lay matters important to the very sovereignty of the new nation. The major proposals in his report recommended that the entire national debt be funded at face value with arrears of interest and that the national government assume the debts that states had incurred in the Revolutionary War.

The national debt included nearly $12 million owed abroad, mainly in France and Holland, and more than $40 million owed to Americans in the United States. There was general agreement about the importance of promptly and fully redeeming the debt held abroad. But there were widespread differences over funding at face value the debt held by Americans. Many of these securities had greatly depreciated, and much of this debt was now in the hands of speculators, who had bought the notes from veterans and others who had been paid for wartime services and supplies with government notes.

The following excerpts from the report focus on Hamilton's opening arguments and proposals for refinancing the national debt. The report fills thirty-four pages in *Documentary History of the First Federal Congress.*

ALEXANDER HAMILTON

Report of the Secretary of the Treasury on the Public Credit

January 14, 1790

TREASURY DEPARTMENT, *January 14, 1790*
The Secretary of the Treasury, in obedience to the resolution of the House of Representatives, of the twenty-first day of September last, has, during the recess of Congress, applied himself to the consideration of a proper plan for the support of the Public Credit, with all the attention which was due to the authority of the House, and to the magnitude of the object.

In the discharge of this duty, he has felt, in no small degree, the anxieties which naturally flow from a just estimate of the difficulty of the task, from a well-founded diffidence of his own qualifications for executing it with success, and from a deep and solemn conviction of the momentous

Extract from *Report of the Secretary of the Treasury to the House of Representatives, Relative to a Provision for the Support of the Public Credit of the United States, in Conformity to a Resolution of the Twenty-first Day of September, 1789.* Presented to the House on Thursday the 14th Day of January, 1790. (Published by Order of the House of Representatives. New York: Francis Childs and John Swaine, 1790.) Reprinted in Linda Grant DePauw, Charlene Bangs Bickford, and Helen E. Veit, eds., *Documentary History of the First Federal Congress of the United States of America,* 14 vols. to date (Baltimore: Johns Hopkins University Press, 1972–98), 5:743–48.

nature of the truth contained in the resolution under which his investigations have been conducted, "That an *adequate* provision for the support of the Public Credit, is a matter of high importance to the honor and prosperity of the United States."

With an ardent desire that his well-meant endeavors may be conducive to the real advantage of the nation, and with the utmost deference to the superior judgment of the House, he now respectfully submits the result of his enquiries and reflections, to their indulgent construction.

In the opinion of the Secretary, the wisdom of the House, in giving their explicit sanction to the proposition which has been stated, cannot but be applauded by all, who will seriously consider, and trace through their obvious consequences, these plain and undeniable truths.

That exigencies are to be expected to occur, in the affairs of nations, in which there will be a necessity for borrowing.

That loans in times of public danger, especially from foreign war, are found an indispensable resource, even to the wealthiest of them.

And that in a country, which, like this, is possessed of little active wealth, or in other words, little monied capital, the necessity for that resource, must, in such emergencies, be proportionably urgent.

And as on the one hand, the necessity for borrowing in particular emergencies cannot be doubted, so on the other, it is equally evident, that to be able to borrow upon *good terms,* it is essential that the credit of a nation should be well established.

For when the credit of a country is in any degree questionable, it never fails to give an extravagant premium, in one shape or another, upon all the loans it has occasion to make. Nor does the evil end here; the same disadvantage must be sustained upon whatever is to be bought on terms of future payment.

From this constant necessity of *borrowing* and *buying dear,* it is easy to conceive how immensely the expences of a nation, in a course of time, will be augmented by an unsound state of the public credit. . . .

If the maintenance of public credit, then, be truly so important, the next enquiry which suggests itself is, by what means it is to be effected? The ready answer to which question is, by good faith, by a punctual performance of contracts. States, like individuals, who observe their engagements, are respected and trusted while the reverse is the fate of those, who pursue an opposite conduct.

Every breach of the public engagements, whether from choice or necessity, is in different degrees hurtful to public credit. When such a necessity does truly exist, the evils of it are only to be palliated by a scrupulous attention, on the part of the government, to carry the violation no farther than the necessity absolutely requires, and to manifest, if the nature of the case admits of it, a sincere disposition to make reparation, whenever circumstances shall permit. . . .

While the observance of that good faith, which is the basis of public credit, is recommended by the strongest inducements of political expediency, it is enforced by considerations of still greater authority. There are arguments for it, which rest on the immutable principles of moral obligation. And in proportion as the mind is disposed to contemplate, in the order of Providence, an intimate connection between public virtue and public happiness, will be its repugnancy to a violation of those principles.

This reflection derives additional strength from the nature of the debt of the United States. It was the price of liberty. The faith of America has been repeatedly pledged for it, and with solemnities, that give peculiar force to the obligation. There is indeed reason to regret that it has not hitherto been kept; that the necessities of the war, conspiring with inexperience in the subjects of finance, produced direct infractions; and that the subsequent period has been a continued scene of negative violation, or non-compliance. But a diminution of this regret arises from the reflection, that the last seven years have exhibited an earnest and uniform effort, on the part of the government of the union, to retrieve the national credit, by doing justice to the creditors of the nation; and that the embarrassments of a defective constitution, which defeated this laudable effort, have ceased.

From this evidence of a favorable disposition, given by the former government, the institution of a new one, cloathed with powers competent to calling forth the resources of the community, has excited correspondent expectations. A general belief, accordingly, prevails, that the credit of the United States will quickly be established on the firm foundation of an effectual provision for the existing debt. The influence, which this has had at home, is witnessed by the rapid increase, that has taken place in the market value of the public securities. From January to November, they rose thirty-three and a third per cent, and from that period to this time, they have risen fifty per cent more. And the intelligence from abroad announces effects proportionably favourable to our national credit and consequence.

It cannot but merit particular attention, that among ourselves the most enlightened friends of good government are those, whose expectations are the highest.

To justify and preserve their confidence; to promote the encreasing respectability of the American name; to answer the calls of justice; to restore landed property to its due value; to furnish new resources both to agriculture and commerce; to cement more closely the union of the states; to add to their security against foreign attack; to establish public order on the basis of an upright and liberal policy. These are the great and invaluable ends to be secured, by a proper and adequate provision, at the present period, for the support of public credit.

To this provision we are invited, not only by the general considerations, which have been noticed, but by others of a more particular nature. It will procure to every class of the community some important advantages, and remove some no less important disadvantages.

The advantage to the public creditors from the increased value of that part of their property which constitutes the public debt, needs no explanation.

But there is a consequence of this, less obvious, though not less true, in which every other citizen is interested. It is a well known fact, that in countries in which the national debt is properly funded, and an object of established confidence, it answers most of the purposes of money. Transfers of stock or public debt are there equivalent to payments in specie; or in other words, stock, in the principal transactions of business, passes current as specie. The same thing would, in all probability happen here, under the like circumstances.

The benefits of this are various and obvious.

First. Trade is extended by it; because there is a larger capital to carry it on, and the merchant can at the same time, afford to trade for smaller profits; as his stock, which, when unemployed, brings him in an interest from the government, serves him also as money, when he has a call for it in his commercial operations.

Secondly. Agriculture and manufactures are also promoted by it: For the like reason, that more capital can be commanded to be employed in both; and because the merchant, whose enterprize in foreign trade, gives to them activity an extension, has greater means for enterprize.

Thirdly. The interest of money will be lowered by it; for this is always in a ratio to the quantity of money, and to the quickness of circulation. This circumstance will enable both the public and individuals to borrow on easier and cheaper terms.

And from the combination of these effects, additional aids will be furnished to labour, to industry, and to arts of every kind.

But these good effects of a public debt are only to be looked for, when, by being well funded, it has acquired an *adequate* and *stable* value. Till then, it has rather a contrary tendency. The fluctuation and insecurity incident to it in an unfunded state, render it a mere commodity, and a precarious one. As such, being only an object of occasional and particular speculation, all the money applied to it is so much diverted from the more useful channels of circulation, for which the thing itself affords no substitute: So that, in fact, one serious inconvenience of an unfunded debt is, that it contributes to the scarcity of money.

This distinction which has been little if at all attended to, is of the greatest moment. It involves a question immediately interesting to every part of the community; which is no other than this — Whether the public debt, by a provision for it on true principles, shall be rendered a *substitute* for money; or whether, by being left as it is, or by being provided for in such a manner as will wound those principles, and destroy confidence, it shall be suffered to continue, as it is, a pernicious drain of our cash from the channels of productive industry.

The effect, which the funding of the public debt, on right principles, would have upon landed property, is one of the circumstances attending such an arrangement, which has been least adverted to, though it deserves the most particular attention. The present depreciated state of that species of property is a serious calamity. The value of cultivated lands, in most of the states, has fallen since the revolution from 25 to 50 per cent. In those farthest south, the decrease is still more considerable. Indeed, if the representations, continually received from that quarter, may be credited, lands there will command no price, which may not be deemed an almost total sacrifice.

This decrease, in the value of lands, ought, in a great measure, to be attributed to the scarcity of money. Consequently whatever produces an augmentation of the monied capital of the country, must have a proportional effect in raising that value. The beneficial tendency of a funded debt, in this respect, has been manifested by the most decisive experience in Great-Britain.

The proprietors of lands would not only feel the benefit of this increase in the value of their property, and of a more prompt and better sale, when they had occasion to sell; but the necessity of selling would be, itself, greatly diminished. As the same cause would contribute to the facility of loans, there is reason to believe, that such of them as are indebted, would be able through that resource, to satisfy their more urgent creditors. . . .

When George Washington chose his cabinet, the general views of Jefferson and Hamilton were well enough known that the president would not have been unaware that he was enlisting advisers with different viewpoints and opinions. He was well aware of Jefferson's agrarian outlook and his faith in the people, and he could sense Hamilton's distrust of the popular will. At the same time, the collaboration of Jefferson's friend James Madison with Hamilton in writing the influential *Federalist* papers, which urged the ratification of the Constitution, would not have led Washington to anticipate the deep divisions that would develop between Jefferson and Hamilton.

As Washington's two closest advisers, Hamilton and Jefferson were thrown together for the first time. The earliest extant letters between the two were exchanged in April 1790.[1] If Jefferson had not seen a copy of Hamilton's *Report on the Public Credit* before he reached New York, he saw it soon after his arrival, for he sent a copy to William Short in Paris on April 6.[2] Matters in his own department, however, demanded Jefferson's first attention. "Much business had been put by for my arrival," Jefferson wrote to his son-in-law Thomas Mann Randolph Jr. a week after he reached New York, "so that I found myself all at once involved under an accumulation of it."[3] Jefferson thus was not immediately drawn into the controversy that Hamilton's report generated in Congress, where Madison, a member of the House from Virginia, was soon differing with his *Federalist* papers collaborator.

While supporting full funding of the debt held abroad, Madison proposed that the domestic debt be redeemed at face value only to original holders. Subsequent purchasers would receive a lesser amount. The proposal posed obvious problems of administration, but the idea found considerable support.

Hamilton's recommendation for the assumption of state debts generated even more opposition than his plan for funding the domestic debt at face value. Some states had made considerable progress in paying their debts, while other states had redeemed few or none of their notes. Madison proposed that if state debts were assumed, the obligations be as of 1783 — the close of the war — rather than as of 1790, as recommended by Hamilton. This would compensate states that had paid down their debts.[4]

Throughout the congressional debates on his report, Hamilton firmly defended his original proposals and was active in building support for them in Congress and outside of the government. Senator William Maclay of Pennsylvania reported from Congress Hall on February 1, 1790, that Hamilton "was here early to wait on the speaker, and I believe spends most of his time in running from place to place among the Members." During the following week, Maclay recorded in his diary that

---

[1] Harold C. Syrett et al., eds., *The Papers of Alexander Hamilton,* 27 vols. (New York: Columbia University Press, 1961–87), 6:368; Julian P. Boyd, Charles T. Cullen, and John Catanzariti, eds., *The Papers of Thomas Jefferson,* 27 vols. to date (Princeton, N.J.: Princeton University Press, 1950–), 16:353.

[2] Jefferson to Short, Apr. 6, 1790, in Boyd, Cullen, and Catanzariti, eds., *Jefferson Papers,* 16:315–17.

[3] Jefferson to Randolph, Mar. 28, 1790, ibid., p. 278.

[4] Ralph Ketcham, *James Madison: A Biography* (New York: Macmillan, 1971), pp. 306–8.

"Hamilton literally speaking is moving heaven and Earth in favour of his System."[5]

When the House became deadlocked over the issues of funding the national debt and assuming state debts, Jefferson played an unexpected role in the final resolution of the issue. Later, probably in 1792, he recorded the following account in a memorandum for his own records.

[5]Kenneth R. Bowling and Helen E. Veit, eds., *The Diary of William Maclay and Other Notes on Senate Debates,* in Linda Grant DePauw, Charlene Bangs Bickford, and Helen E. Veit, eds., *Documentary History of the First Federal Congress of the United States of America,* 14 vols. (Baltimore: John Hopkins University Press, 1972–98), 9:195, 200.

THOMAS JEFFERSON

Account of a Compromise on Assumption and Residence Bills

[1792]

The assumption of the state debts in 1790 was a supplementary measure in Hamilton's fiscal system. When attempted in the House of Representatives it failed. This threw Hamilton himself and a number of members into deep dismay. Going to the President's one day I met Hamilton as I approached the door. His look was sombre, haggard, and dejected beyond description. Even his dress uncouth and neglected. He asked to speak with me. We stood in the street near the door. He opened the subject of the assumption of the state debts, the necessity of it in the general fiscal arrangement and it's indispensible necessity towards a preservation of the union: and particularly of the New England states, who had made great expenditures during the war, on expeditions which tho' of their own undertaking were for the common cause: that they considered the assumption of these by the Union so just, and it's denial so palpably injurious, that they would make it a sine qua non of a continuance of the Union. That as to his own part, if he had not credit enough to carry such a measure as that, he could be of no use, and was determined to resign. He observed at the same time, that tho' our particular business laid in separate departments, yet the administration and it's success was a common concern, and that we

Julian P. Boyd, Charles T. Cullen, and John Catanzariti, eds., *The Papers of Thomas Jefferson.* 27 vols. to date (Princeton: Princeton University Press, 1950–), 17:205–8.

should make common cause in supporting one another. He added his wish that I would interest my friends from the South, who were those most opposed to it. I answered that I had been so long absent from my country that I had lost a familiarity with it's affairs, and being but lately returned had not yet got into the train of them, that the fiscal system being out of my department, I had not yet undertaken to consider and understand it, that the assumption had struck me in an unfavorable light, but still not having considered it sufficiently I had not concerned in it, but that I would resolve what he had urged in my mind. It was a real fact that the Eastern and Southern members (S. Carolina however was with the former) had got into the most extreme ill humor with one another, this broke out on every question with the most alarming heat, the bitterest animosities seemed to be engendered, and tho' they met every day, little or nothing could be done from mutual distrust and antipathy. On considering the situation of things I thought the first step towards some conciliation of views would be to bring Mr. Madison and Colo. Hamilton to a friendly discussion of the subject. I immediately wrote to each to come and dine with me the next day, mentioning that we should be alone, that the object was to find some temperament for the present fever, and that I was persuaded that men of sound heads and honest views needed nothing more than explanation and mutual understanding to enable them to unite in some measures which might enable us to get along. They came. I opened the subject to them, acknoleged that my situation had not permitted me to understand it sufficiently but encouraged them to consider the thing together. They did so. It ended in Mr. Madison's acquiescence in a proposition that the question should be again brought before the house by way of amendment from the Senate, that tho' he would not vote for it, nor entirely withdraw his opposition, yet he should not be strenuous, but leave it to it's fate. It was observed, I forget by which of them, that as the pill would be a bitter one to the Southern states, something should be done to soothe them; that the removal of the seat of government to the Patowmac[6] was a just measure, and would probably be a popular one with them, and would be a proper one to follow the assumption. It was agreed to speak to Mr. White[7] and Mr. Lee,[8] whose districts lay on the Patowmac and to refer to them to consider how far the interests of their particular districts might be a sufficient inducement to them to yield to the assumption. This was done. Lee came into it without hesitation. Mr. White had some qualms, but finally agreed. The measure came down by way of amendment from the Senate and was finally carried by the change of White's and Lee's votes. But the removal to Patowmac could not be carried unless Pennsylvania could be engaged

---

[6] Patowmac: Potomac River.
[7] Representative Alexander White of Virginia.
[8] Representative Richard Bland Lee of Virginia.

in it. This Hamilton took on himself, and chiefly, as I understood, through the agency of Robert Morris,[9] obtained the vote of that state, on agreeing to an intermediate residence at Philadelphia. This is the real history of the assumption, about which many erroneous conjectures have been published. It was unjust, in itself oppressive to the states, and was acquiesced in merely from a fear of disunion, while our government was still in it's most infant state. It enabled Hamilton so to strengthen himself by corrupt services to many, that he could afterwards carry his bank scheme, and every measure he proposed in defiance of all opposition: in fact it was a principal ground whereon was reared up that Speculating phalanx, in and out of Congress which has since been able to give laws and to change the political complexion of the government of the US.

By July 1790, a compromise along the lines described by Jefferson was worked out, and Congress passed legislation for funding the national debt, assuming state debts, and locating the permanent seat of government on the Potomac River. As part of the agreement, the temporary capital was moved to Philadelphia for ten years. Not all of the compromises and provisions of the agreement had been worked out at Jefferson's dinner table. Indeed, some understanding between southern members and Pennsylvanians may have been reached before the dinner. When Jefferson looked back on the bargain much later, he came to regret his role and to feel that he had been duped by Hamilton and made a tool for forwarding schemes that he did not fully understand. In the summer of 1790, however, Jefferson's differences with Hamilton were not as sharp as they would soon become, and he saw compromise as necessary to preserve the new union under the Constitution.[10] "I see the necessity of sacrificing our opinions sometimes to the opinions of others for the sake of harmony," he wrote to his son-in-law Francis Eppes on July 4, 1790.[11]

While Hamilton's *Report on the Public Credit* was dominating the attention of Congress and the public, Jefferson was occupied with a press-

---

[9] Senator Robert Morris of Pennsylvania.

[10] Noble E. Cunningham Jr., *In Pursuit of Reason: The Life of Thomas Jefferson* (Baton Rouge: Louisiana State University Press, 1987), p. 140; Jacob E. Cooke, "The Compromise of 1790," *William and Mary Quarterly*, 3rd Ser., 27 (1971):523–45; Kenneth R. Bowling, "Dinner at Jefferson's," *William and Mary Quarterly*, 3rd Ser., 28 (1971):629–40.

[11] Boyd, Cullen, and Catanzariti, eds., *Jefferson Papers*, 16:598.

ing assignment to prepare "a proper plan or plans for establishing uniformity in the Currency, Weights, and Measures of the United States."[12] This task had been assigned to the secretary of state as an official duty on January 15, 1790, before Jefferson's arrival in New York. It was an assignment that Jefferson found intellectually exciting, and he plunged into the task with high interest and intensity, despite suffering from one of his periodic disabling headaches. In editing Jefferson's papers, Julian Boyd concluded that Madison was a close collaborator in drafting the plan but that the result was essentially Jefferson's own, "embracing the advanced opinion of men of learning in Europe and in America."[13] Jefferson proposed to apply the decimal system to weights and measures, just as Congress had done earlier under the Confederation, at his recommendation, in regard to coinage. He sent a copy of his report to Hamilton, who replied that he had perused it "with much satisfaction" and agreed that "the idea of a general standard among nations . . . seems full of convenience and order."[14] Congress was not prepared to take the far-reaching steps that Jefferson proposed, however, and failed to act on his proposal, leaving it to revolutionary France to initiate the metric system.

Jefferson's attention was soon occupied with more pressing matters than the system of weights and measures, as he faced his first major challenge in foreign affairs as secretary of state. In this crisis, Hamilton would become involved to an extent unknown to Jefferson. The occasion was the threat of a war between England and Spain following the Spanish seizure of British ships in Nootka Sound off Vancouver Island. Should Great Britain attempt the conquest of Louisiana and the Floridas, the conflict would most directly threaten the interests of the United States in the navigation of the Mississippi River. In the absence of any diplomatic mission to the United States, unofficial contacts were made between Major George Beckwith — a British intelligence officer and aide to Lord Dorchester, the governor-general of Canada — and Alexander Hamilton.[15] Jefferson and Washington were informed of Hamilton's

---

[12] Ibid., pp. 604–5.
[13] Ibid., p. 614.
[14] Hamilton to Jefferson, June 16, 1790, ibid., pp. 511–12.
[15] Julian P. Boyd, *Number 7: Alexander Hamilton's Secret Attempts to Control American Foreign Policy* (Princeton: Princeton University Press, 1964), pp. xiii–xiv; Stanley

conversations with Beckwith, which were reported and discussed at a meeting on July 8, 1790.[16] But Hamilton's memorandum to the president did not contain all of the information found in Beckwith's report to Lord Dorchester. Beckwith reported to Dorchester that Hamilton assured him that

> there is the most sincere good disposition on the part of the government here to go into the consideration of all matters unsettled between us and Great Britain, in order to effect a perfect understanding between the two countries, and to lay the foundation for future amity; this, particularly as it respects commercial objects, we view as conducive to our interest.
>
> In the present stage of this business it is difficult to say much on the subject of a Treaty of Alliance; Your rupture with Spain, if it shall take place, opens a very wide political field; thus much I can say, we are perfectly unconnected with Spain, have even some points unadjusted with that Court, and are prepared to go into the consideration of the subject.[17]

Both Washington and Jefferson favored the negotiation of a commercial treaty with Great Britain and were also ready to use the crisis to press Spain for concessions, but Beckwith's report of his interview with Hamilton indicated a more conciliatory stance than that taken by either the president or the secretary of state. In his conversation with Beckwith, Hamilton urged that negotiations take place in the United States rather than in London. Beckwith also noted in his report to Lord Dorchester that Hamilton indicated his willingness to intervene if difficulties with Jefferson developed. He reported that Hamilton said,

> If it shall be judged proper to proceed in this business by the sending or appointing a proper person to come to this country to negotiate on the spot, whoever shall then be Our Secretary of State, will be the person in whose department such negotiation must originate, and he will be the channel of communication with the President; in the turn of such affairs the most minute circumstances, mere trifles, give a favorable bias or otherwise to the whole. The President's mind I can declare to be perfectly dispassionate of this subject. Mr. Jefferson our present Secretary of State is I am persuaded a gentleman of honor, and zealously desirous of promoting those objects, which the nature of his duty calls for, and the interests

---

Elkins and Eric McKitrick, *The Age of Federalism: The American Republic, 1788–1800* (New York: Oxford University Press, 1993), pp. 124–26.

[16] Donald Jackson and Dorothy Twohig, eds., *The Diaries of George Washington*, 6 vols. (Charlottesville: University Press of Virginia, 1976–79), 6:87–89; Syrett et al., eds., *Hamilton Papers*, 6:484–86.

[17] Syrett et al., eds., *Hamilton Papers*, 6:496.

of his country may require, but from some opinions which he has given respecting Your government, and possible predilections elsewhere, there may be difficulties which may possibly frustrate the whole, and which might be readily explained away. I shall certainly know the progress of negotiation from the president from day to day, but what I come to the present explanation for is this, that in any case any such difficulties should occur, I should wish to know them, in order that I may be sure they are clearly understood, and candidly examined, if none takes place the business will of course go on in the regular channel.[18]

Without Jefferson's knowledge, Hamilton was offering to assist the representative of a foreign power in negotiations with the secretary of state. As it turned out, the war crisis ended when France failed to support Spain in the Nootka Sound dispute and Spain came to terms with Great Britain. Contact between Hamilton and Beckwith, nevertheless, continued. Hamilton had at least three more conversations with Beckwith before the Treasury Department moved to Philadelphia in late October 1790.[19] Only two of these were reported to the president, who was at Mount Vernon, and there is no record of any of the contacts being reported to Jefferson, who was at Monticello.

Colonel Beckwith, having been promoted, was in Philadelphia during several months in 1791, and he again engaged in conversations with Hamilton and others.[20] Jefferson was not among them, for as secretary of state, he would talk to no unofficial agent of a foreign power. Jefferson did, however, ask Madison to talk to Beckwith, and Madison provided him with a full report.[21] By this time, relations between Jefferson and Hamilton were becoming increasingly distant, as Jefferson more and more championed ideas and policies opposed to those of the secretary of the Treasury.

Historians who have studied the growing differences between Jefferson and Hamilton at this stage of their public careers have often come to divergent assessments of the two statesmen. Dumas Malone, author of the most extensive biography of Jefferson, presented a contrasting portrait of Jefferson and Hamilton in the introduction to the second volume

---

[18] Secret conversation with George Beckwith, July 15, 1790, ibid., p. 497.

[19] Ibid., 7:70–74, 84–85.

[20] Ibid., 8:41–45, 342–43, 475–77, 544–46, 9:29–30.

[21] Jefferson to Madison, Mar. 13, 1791; Madison, memorandum to Jefferson [ca. Apr. 18, 1791], in William T. Hutchinson et al., eds., *The Papers of James Madison,* 17 vols. (Charlottesville: University Press of Virginia, 1962–91), 13:404–5, 14:7–10.

of his five-volume work. Broadus Mitchell, author of a two-volume biography of Hamilton, also offered a comparative assessment of the two statesmen.

DUMAS MALONE

Assessment of Thomas Jefferson and Alexander Hamilton
1951

Jefferson . . . has withstood microscopic examination even better than I expected. This is not to claim that his judgment was always right, but no one can read his voluminous state papers without gaining increased respect for his ability, and, considering the enormous body of personal papers he left, they show amazingly few spots on his character. His chief weakness . . . was a defect of his politeness and amiability which caused him to seem deceptive. This was also a reflection of an extreme distaste for personal controversy. With the possible exception of Washington, he was the most sensitive of the major public men of his era, and he was far more disposed to battle for principles and policies than for his own interests. Perhaps that is the real secret of his eventual political success, as it assuredly is of his enduring fame. He was a true and pure symbol of the rights of man because, in his own mind, the cause was greater than himself. . . .

I am sorry to say, Hamilton comes out of my investigations worse than I had expected. No reader need accept any of my judgments, but they are based on the fairest reading that I could give the records of the time, including Hamilton's own writings. It has been said before now that he was his own worst enemy, and I believe that his own words . . . clearly prove it. As I have lived through these events in spirit my wonderment has been, not that Jefferson resented the words and actions of his brilliant, egotistical, and overbearing colleague, but that he maintained so long an attitude of impersonality and was so slow to anger. I have tried to judge Hamilton's bold policies on their merits, but I cannot escape the conviction that he, more than any other major American statesman of his time, lusted for personal as well as national power.

Dumas Malone, *Jefferson and the Rights of Man,* vol. 2 of *Jefferson and His Time* (Boston: Little, Brown, 1948–81), pp. xxi–xxii.

Assessment of Alexander Hamilton and Thomas Jefferson

1962

The differences that developed between Jefferson and Hamilton were due partly to contrasts of temperament, environment, background, and experience. The trouble sprang also from the momentum with which Hamilton entered on the national enterprise as compared with the lethargy and distaste of Jefferson. Hamilton, on the ground, had worked for years for this very opportunity — removing obstacles, forwarding constructive measures, anticipating next problems, and providing solutions. This was the purpose that possessed him. Not only his mind but his heart was in it. He was in love with the noble ideal of creating a vigorous, expanding nation. Nothing was too difficult or interfered too much with his private concerns. He exerted himself in this behalf not from a sense of duty, nor with an eye to his own fame, but from a consuming affection. This was his own fulfillment.

Jefferson, on the other hand, had just returned from years abroad, did not know the game in this country or the roles played by different actors in his long absence. He had come from a scene of decay which was to be swept off the boards by political and physical violence. With this apocalypse he had sympathized; indeed, to it he had contributed, not indigenously, but as an outsider, a world evangel. He heard voices, saw visions, but was far from the stage of devising institutions or finding ways and means of equipping a new social order. The France that he had left was far behind America in political progress, was in a seizure of revelation and revolution from which she would be long in emerging. Jefferson was tired and homesick, and home to him meant not the national capital, not fresh involvement in affairs of state, but his rural retreat of Monticello, his farm, his library, his family.

Broadus Mitchell, *Alexander Hamilton: The National Adventure, 1788–1804* (New York: Macmillan, 1962), pp. 206–7.

Figure 3. *Alexander Hamilton.*
Oil portrait painted from life by Charles Willson Peale, circa 1791.
Independence National Historical Park Collection, Philadelphia.

3

Poles Apart on Banks and Factories

During the fall of 1790, the offices of government of the United States moved from New York to Philadelphia. Alexander Hamilton was at the Treasury Department's new office by late October. Meanwhile, President Washington remained at Mount Vernon, and Thomas Jefferson was at Monticello. Traveling with Congressman James Madison, Jefferson reached Philadelphia on November 20, a week before the president arrived in the new capital.

A few days after Madison took up residence again at Mrs. Mary House's boardinghouse in Philadelphia, Hamilton sent him the draft of his *Report on the Further Provision Necessary for Establishing Public Credit.* Asking the congressman to peruse the report, Hamilton promised to call on him the next day, weather permitting, to discuss it.[1] He also asked Madison to pass the paper on to Jefferson.

Hamilton did not finish the second of his two reports on further provisions necessary for establishing public credit until December 13, 1790, the day before submitting it to Congress, and he did not share this report with either Madison or Jefferson.[2] In the second report, Hamilton proposed the establishment of a national bank, arguing that such an institution would be "of primary importance to the prosperous administration of the Finances, and would be of the greater utility in the operations connected with the support of the Public Credit."[3]

Hamilton's report reflected emulation of the Bank of England, a key component of England's emerging capitalism. Anticipating opposition

---

[1] Hamilton to Madison, Nov. 24, [1790?], in William T. Hutchinson et al., eds., *The Papers of James Madison,* 17 vols. (Chicago and Charlottesville: University Press of Virginia, 1962–91), 13:306. Hamilton's note could have been written in 1791, but the editors of the *Madison Papers* make a convincing case for 1790.

[2] Harold C. Syrett et al., eds., *The Papers of Alexander Hamilton,* 27 vols. (New York: Columbia University Press, 1961–87), 7:236, 305.

[3] Ibid., p. 305.

from Francophiles and agrarians like Jefferson — and also Madison — Hamilton confronted their fears and also the American public's hostility to the former mother country. Hamilton began his report with an exposition on the advantages of banks.

ALEXANDER HAMILTON

Report on a National Bank

December 14, 1790

It is a fact well understood, that public Banks have found admission and patronage among the principal and most enlightened commercial nations. They have successively obtained in Italy, Germany, Holland, England and France, as well as in the United States. And it is a circumstance, which cannot but have considerable weight, in a candid estimate of their tendency, that after an experience of centuries, there exists not a question about their util[ity] in the countries in which they have been so long established. Theorists and men of business unite in the acknowlegment of it.

Trade and industry, wherever they have been tried, have been indebted to them for important aid. And Government has been repeatedly under the greatest obligations to them, in dangerous and distressing emergencies. That of the United States, as well in some of the most critical conjunctures of the late war, as since the peace, has received assistance from those established among us, with which it could not have dispensed. . . .

The following are among the principal advantages of a Bank.

First. The augmentation of the active or productive capital of a country. Gold and Silver, when they are employed merely as the instruments of exchange and alienation, have been not improperly denominated dead Stock; but when deposited in Banks, to become the basis of a paper circulation, which takes their character and place, as the signs or representatives of value, they then acquire life, or, in other words, an active and productive quality. This idea, which appears rather subtil and abstract, in a general form, may be made obvious and palpable, by entering into a few particulars. It is evident, for instance, that the money, which a merchant keeps in his chest, waiting for a favourable opportunity to employ it, produces nothing 'till that opportunity arrives. But if instead of locking it up in this manner, he either deposits it in a Bank, or invests it in the Stock of a Bank, it yields a profit, during the interval; in which he partakes, or not,

Harold C. Syrett et al., eds., *The Papers of Alexander Hamilton,* 27 vols. (New York: Columbia University Press, 1961–87), 7:306–11.

according to the choice he may have made of being a depositor or a proprietor; and when any advantageous speculation offers, in order to be able to embrace it, he has only to withdraw his money, if a depositor, or if a proprietor to obtain a loan from the Bank, or to dispose of his Stock; an alternative seldom or never attended with difficulty, when the affairs of the institution are in a prosperous train. His money thus deposited or invested, is a fund, upon which himself and others can borrow to a much larger amount. It is a well established fact, that Banks in good credit can circulate a far greater sum than the actual quantum of their capital in Gold & Silver. The extent of the possible excess seems indeterminate; though it has been conjecturally stated at the proportions of two and three to one. This faculty is produced in various ways. First. A great proportion of the notes, which are issued and pass current as Cash, are indefinitely suspended in circulation, from the confidence which each holder has, that he can at any moment turn them into gold and silver. Secondly, Every loan, which a Bank makes is, in its first shape, a credit given to the borrower on its books, the amount of which it stands ready to pay, either in its own notes, or in gold or silver, at his option. But, in a great number of cases, no actual payment is made in either. The Borrower frequently, by a check or order, transfers his credit to some other person, to whom he has a payment to make; who, in his turn, is as often content with a similar credit, because he is satisfied, that he can, whenever he pleases, either convert it into cash, or pass it to some other hand, as an equivalent for it. And in this manner the credit keeps circulating, performing in every stage the office of money, till it is extinguished by a discount with some person, who has a payment to make to the Bank, to an equal or greater amount. Thus large sums are lent and paid, frequently through a variety of hands, without the intervention of a single piece of coin. Thirdly, There is always a large quantity of gold and silver in the repositories of the Bank, besides its own Stock, which is placed there, with a view partly to its safe keeping and partly to the accommodation of an institution, which is itself a source of general accommodation. These deposits are of immense consequence in the operations of a Bank. Though liable to be redrawn at any moment, experience proves, that the money so much oftener changes proprietors than place, and that what is drawn out is generally so speedily replaced, as to authorise the counting upon the sums deposited, as an *effective fund;* which, concurring with the Stock of the Bank, enables it to extend its loans, and to answer all the demands for coin, whether in consequence of those loans, or arising from the occasional return of its notes.

These different circumstances explain the manner, in which the ability of a bank to circulate a greater sum, than its actual capital in coin, is acquired. This however must be gradual; and must be preceded by a firm establishment of confidence; a confidence which may be bestowed on the most rational grounds; since the excess in question will always be bottomed on good security of one kind or another. This, every well conducted Bank carefully requires, before it will consent to advance either its money or its credit; and where there is an auxiliary capital (as will be the case in the plan hereafter submitted) which, together with the capital in coin, define the boundary, that shall not be exceeded by the engagements of the Bank, the security may, consistently with all the maxims of a reasonable circumspection be regarded as complete.

The same circumstances illustrate the truth of the position, that it is one of the properties of Banks to increase the active capital of a country. This, in other words is the sum of them. The money of one individual, while he is waiting for an opportunity to employ it, by being either deposited in the Bank for safe keeping, or invested in its Stock, is in a condition to administer to the wants of others, without being put out of his own reach, when occasion presents. This yields an extra profit, arising from what is paid for the use of his money by others, when he could not himself make use of it; and keeps the money itself in a state of incessant activity. In the almost infinite vicissitudes and competitions of mercantile enterprise, there never can be danger of an intermission of demand, or that the money will remain for a moment idle in the vaults of the Bank. This additional employment given to money, and the faculty of a bank to lend and circulate a greater sum than the amount of its stock in coin are to all the purposes of trade and industry an absolute increase of capital. Purchases and undertakings, in general, can be carried on by any given sum of bank paper or credit, as effectually as by an equal sum of gold and silver. And thus by contributing to enlarge the mass of industrious and commercial enterprise, banks become nurseries of national wealth: a consequence, as satisfactorily verified by experience, as it is clearly deducible in theory.

Secondly. Greater facility to the Government in obtaining pecuniary aids, especially in sudden emergencies. This is another and an undisputed advantage of public banks: one, which as already remarked, has been realised in signal instances, among ourselves. The reason is obvious: The capitals of a great number of individuals are, by this operation, collected to a point, and placed under one direction. The mass, formed by this union, is in a certain sense magnified by the credit attached to it: And while this mass is always ready, and can at once be put in motion, in aid of the Government, the interest of the bank to afford that aid, independent of regard to the public safety and welfare, is a sure pledge for its disposition to go as far as its compliances, as can in prudence be desired. There is in the nature of things, as will be more particularly noticed in another place, an intimate connection of interest between the government and the Bank of a Nation.

Thirdly. The facilitating of the payment of taxes. This advantage is produced in two ways. Those who are in a situation to have access to the Bank can have the assistance of loans to answer with punctuality the public calls upon them. This accommodation has been sensibly felt in the payment of the duties heretofore laid, by those who reside where establishments of this nature exist. This however, though an extensive, is not an universal benefit. The other way, in which the effect here contemplated is produced, and in which the benefit is general, is the encreasing of the quantity of circulating medium and the quickening of circulation. The manner in which the first happens has already been traced. The last may require some illustration. When payments are to be made between different places, having an intercourse of business with each other, if there happen to be no private bills, at market, and there are no Bank notes, which have a currency in both, the consequence is, that coin must be remitted. This is attended with trouble, delay, expence and risk. If on the contrary, there are bank notes current in both places, the transmission of these by the post, or any other speedy, or convenient conveyance answers the purpose; and these again, in the alternations of demand, are frequently returned, very soon after, to the place from whence they were first sent: Whence the transportation and retransportation of the metals are obviated; and a more convenient and more expeditious medium of payment is substituted. Nor is this all. The metals, instead of being suspended from their usual functions, during this process of vibration from place to place, continue in activity, and administer still to the ordinary circulation; which of course is prevented from suffering either diminution or stagnation. These circumstances are additional causes of what, in a practical sense, or to the purposes of business, may be called greater plenty of money. And it is evident, that whatever enhances the quantity of circulating money adds to the ease, with which every industrious member of the community may acquire that portion of it, of which he stands in need; and enables him the better to pay his taxes, as well as to supply his other wants. Even where the circulation of the bank paper is not general, it must still have the same effect, though in a less degree. For whatever furnishes additional supplies to the channels of circulation, in one quarter, naturally contributes to keep the streams fuller elsewhere. This last view of the subject serves both to illustrate the position, that Banks tend to facilitate the payment of taxes; and to exemplify their utility to business of every kind, in which money is an agent. . . .

Hamilton followed this with an extended examination of arguments against banks, returned to the advantages that banks provided, and concluded with a specific plan for a national bank.[4] At the time Hamilton sent this plan to Congress, Jefferson was so pressed by the demands of the State Department that he could not give much attention to Hamilton's proposal. "Unremitting business since the meeting of Congress has

[4] Ibid., pp. 334–37.

obliged me to a rigorous suspension of my correspondence, and this is the first day I find myself at liberty to resume them," Jefferson wrote on February 4, 1791, replying to a letter of December 10 from Robert R. Livingston, chancellor of New York State. Jefferson did not mention the bank, but he asked the New Yorker, "Are the people in your quarter as well contented with the proceedings of our government, as their representatives say they are?" Then he added that there was "a vast mass of discontent gathered in the South."[5]

Jefferson expressed similar feelings when writing to George Mason, who had been a Virginia delegate to the federal Constitutional Convention, asking Mason, "What is said in our country of the fiscal arrangements now going on?" Predicting that an excise tax and the bank bill would both pass, he suggested that the only corrective would be to increase the numbers in the House of Representatives "to get a more agricultural representation, which may put that interest above that of the stock-jobbers."[6]

On February 8, 1791, the day after the bill to charter the Bank of the United States passed the House of Representatives by a vote of 39 to 20, Jefferson wrote to a Virginia friend that there were objections that Congress had transcended its powers. He surely had Hamilton in mind when he wrote, "There are certainly persons in all the departments who are for driving too fast." Then he added, "Government being founded on opinion, the opinion of the public, even when it is wrong, ought to be respected to a certain degree. The prudence of the President is an anchor of safety to us."[7]

Before the bill to charter the bank was sent to the president on February 12, 1791, Washington had begun to collect the opinions of his advisers on its constitutionality, asking both Attorney General Edmund Randolph and Jefferson for their views. After receiving their opinions, the president enclosed them in a letter to the secretary of the Treasury on February 16, 1791.[8] Hamilton was thus able to address the arguments of both Randolph and Jefferson, though it was Jefferson's reasoning to which Hamilton primarily directed his disquisition.

[5] Julian P. Boyd, Charles T. Cullen, and John Catanzariti, eds., *The Papers of Thomas Jefferson,* 27 vols. to date (Princeton: Princeton University Press, 1950–), 19:240–41.
[6] Jefferson to Mason, Feb. 4, 1791, ibid., pp. 241–42.
[7] Jefferson to Nicholas Lewis, Feb. 9, 1791, ibid., p. 263.
[8] Syrett et al., eds., *Hamilton Papers,* 8:97n.

In an opinion concluding that the proposed bank was unconstitutional, Jefferson reasoned that the Constitution must be rigidly inter-
preted — an argument that came to be identified as "strict construction."
In reply, Hamilton argued for the constitutionality of Congress's power
to charter a national bank, expounding the doctrine of implied powers,
or "loose construction." The arguments presented in these papers became central in the political and constitutional history of the United
States.

THOMAS JEFFERSON

Opinion on the Constitutionality
of Establishing a National Bank

February 15, 1791

. . . I consider the foundation of the Constitution as laid on this ground
that 'all powers not delegated to the U.S. by the Constitution, not prohibited by it to the states, are reserved to the states or to the people' [Xth.
Amendmt.]. To take a single step beyond the boundaries thus specially
drawn around the power of Congress, is to take possession of a boundless
feild of power, no longer susceptible of any definition.

The incorporation of a bank, and other powers assumed by this bill
have not, in my opinion, been delegated to the U.S. by the Constitution.

I. They are not among the powers specially enumerated, for these are

1. A power to *lay taxes* for the purpose of paying the debts of the U.S.
But no debt is paid by this bill, nor any tax laid. Were it a bill to raise
money, it's origination in the Senate would condemn it by the constitution.

2. 'to borrow money.' But this bill neither borrows money, nor ensures
the borrowing it. The proprietors of the bank will be just as free as any
other money holders, to lend or not to lend their money to the public. The
operation proposed in the bill, first to lend them two millions, and then
borrow them back again, cannot change the nature of the latter act, which
will still be a payment, and not a loan, call it by what name you please.

3. 'to regulate commerce with foreign nations, and among the states,
and with the Indian tribes.' To erect a bank, and to regulate commerce, are
very different acts. He who erects a bank creates a subject of commerce in

Julian P. Boyd, Charles T. Cullen, and John Catanzariti, eds., *The Papers of Thomas Jefferson,* 27 vols. to date (Princeton: Princeton University Press, 1950–), 19:275–80.

it's bills: so does he who makes a bushel of wheat, or digs a dollar out of the mines. Yet neither of these persons regulates commerce thereby. To erect a thing which may be bought and sold, is not to prescribe regulations for buying and selling. Besides; if this was an exercise of the power of regulating commerce, it would be void, as extending as much to the internal commerce of every state, as to it's external. For the power given to Congress by the Constitution, does not extend to the internal regulation of the commerce of a state (that is to say of the commerce between citizen and citizen) which remains exclusively with it's own legislature; but to it's external commerce only, that is to say, it's commerce with another state, or with foreign nations or with the Indian tribes. Accordingly the bill does not propose the measure as a 'regulation of trade,' but as 'productive of considerable advantage to trade.'

Still less are these powers covered by any other of the special enumerations.

II. Nor are they within either of the general phrases, which are the two following.

1. 'To lay taxes to provide for the general welfare of the U.S.' that is to say 'to lay taxes *for the purpose* of providing for the general welfare'. For the laying of taxes is the *power* and the general welfare the *purpose* for which the power is to be exercised. They are not to lay taxes ad libitum *for any purpose they please;* but only to *pay the debts or provide for the welfare of the Union.* In like manner they are not *to do anything they please* to provide for the general welfare, but only *to lay taxes* for that purpose. To consider the latter phrase, not as describing the purpose of the first, but as giving a distinct and independent power to do any act they please, which might be for the good of the Union, would render all the preceding and subsequent enumerations of power completely useless. It would reduce the whole instrument to a single phrase, that of instituting a Congress with power to do whatever would be for the good of the U.S. and as they would be the sole judges of the good or evil, it would be also a power to do whatever evil they pleased. It is an established rule of construction, where a phrase will bear either of two meanings, to give it that which will allow some meaning to the other parts of the instrument, and not that which would render all the others useless. Certainly no such universal power was meant to be given them. It was intended to lace them up straitly within the enumerated powers, and those without which, as means, these powers could not be carried into effect. It is known that the very power now proposed *as a means,* was rejected *as an end,* by the Convention which formed the constitution. A proposition was made to them to authorize Congress to open canals, and an amendatory one to empower them to incorporate. But the whole was rejected, and one of the reasons of rejection urged in debate was that then they would have a power to erect a bank, which would render the great cities, where there were prejudices and jealousies on that subject adverse to the reception of the constitution.

2. The second general phrase is 'to make all laws *necessary* and proper for carrying into execution the enumerated powers.' But they can all be carried into execution without a bank. A bank therefore is not *necessary,* and consequently not authorised by this phrase.

It has been much urged that a bank will give great facility, or convenience in the collection of taxes. Suppose this were true: yet the constitution allows only the means which are 'necessary' not those which are merely 'convenient' for effecting the enumerated powers. If such a latitude of construction be allowed to this phrase as to give any non-enumerated power, it will go to every one, for there is no one which ingenuity may not torture into a *convenience, in some way or other,* to *some one* of so long a list of enumerated powers. It would swallow up all the delegated powers, and reduce the whole to one phrase as before observed. Therefore it was that the constitution restrained them to the *necessary* means, that is to say, to those means without which the grant of the power would be nugatory.

But let us examine this *convenience,* and see what it is. The report on this subject, page 3. states the only *general* convenience to be the preventing the transportation and re-transportation of money between the states and the treasury. (For I pass over the increase of circulating medium ascribed to it as a merit, and which, according to my ideas of paper money is clearly a demerit.) Every state will have to pay a sum of tax-money into the treasury: and the treasury will have to pay, in every state, a part of the interest on the public debt, and salaries to the officers of government resident in that state. In most of the states there will still be a surplus of tax-money to come up to the seat of government for the officers residing there. The payments of interest and salary in each state may be made by treasury-orders on the state collector. This will take up the greater part of the money he has collected in his state, and consequently prevent the great mass of it from being drawn out of the state. If there be a balance of commerce in favour of that state against the one in which the government resides, the surplus of taxes will be remitted by the bills of exchange drawn for that commercial balance. And so it must be if there was a bank. But if there be no balance of commerce, either direct or circuitous, all the banks in the world could not bring up the surplus of taxes but in the form of money. Treasury orders then and bills of exchange may prevent the displacement of the main mass of the money collected, without the aid of any bank: and where these fail, it cannot be prevented even with that aid.

Perhaps indeed bank bills may be a more *convenient* vehicle than treasury orders. But a little *difference* in the degree of *convenience,* cannot constitute the necessity which the constitution makes the ground for assuming any non-enumerated power.

Besides; the existing banks will without a doubt, enter into arrangements for lending their agency: and the more favourable, as there will be a competition among them for it: whereas the bill delivers us up bound to the national bank, who are free to refuse all arrangement, but on their own terms, and the public not free, on such refusal, to employ any other bank. That of Philadelphia, I believe, now does this business, by their post-notes, which by an arrangement with the treasury, are paid by any state collector to whom they are presented. This expedient alone suffices to prevent the existence of that *necessity* which may justify the assumption of a non-enumerated power as a means for carrying into effect an enumerated one. The thing may be done, and has been done, and well done without this assumption; therefore it does not stand on that degree of *necessity* which can honestly justify it.

It may be said that a bank, whose bills would have a currency all over the states, would be more convenient than one whose currency is limited to a single state. So it would be still more convenient that there should be a bank whose bills should have a currency all over the world. But it does not follow from this superior convenience that there exists anywhere a power to establish such a bank; or that the world may not go on very well without it. . . .

The Negative of the President is the shield provided by the constitution to protect against the invasions of the legislature 1. the rights of the Executive 2. of the Judiciary 3. of the states and state legislatures. The present is the case of a right remaining exclusively with the states and is consequently one of those intended by the constitution to be placed under his protection.

It must be added however, that unless the President's mind on a view of every thing which is urged for and against this bill, is tolerably clear that it is unauthorised by the constitution, if the pro and the con hang so even as to balance his judgment, a just respect for the wisdom of the legislature would naturally decide the balance in favour of their opinion. It is chiefly for cases where they are clearly misled by error, ambition, or interest, that the constitution has placed a check in the negative of the President.

TH: JEFFERSON
Feb. 15. 1791.

Opinion on the Constitutionality
of Establishing a National Bank

February 23, 1791

The Secretary of the Treasury having perused with attention the papers containing the opinions of the Secretary of State and Attorney General concerning the constitutionality of the bill for establishing a National Bank proceeds according to the order of the President to submit the reasons which have induced him to entertain a different opinion.

It will naturally have been anticipated that, in performing this task he would feel uncommon solicitude. Personal considerations alone arising from the reflection that the measure originated with him would be sufficient to produce it: The sense which he has manifested of the great importance of such an institution to the successful administration of the department under his particular care; and an expectation of serious ill consequences to result from a failure of the measure, do not permit him to be without anxiety on public accounts. But the chief solicitude arises from a firm persuasion, that principles of construction like those espoused by the Secretary of State and the Attorney General would be fatal to the just & indispensible authority of the United States.

In entering upon the argument it ought to be premised, that the objections of the Secretary of State and Attorney General are founded on a general denial of the authority of the United States to erect corporations. The latter indeed expressly admits, that if there be any thing in the bill which is not warranted by the constitution, it is the clause of incorporation.

Now it appears to the Secretary of the Treasury, that this *general principle is inherent* in the very *definition* of *Government* and *essential* to every step of the progress to be made by that of the United States; namely — that every power vested in a Government is in its nature *sovereign,* and includes by *force* of the *term,* a right to employ all the *means* requisite, and fairly *applicable* to the attainment of the *ends* of such power; and which are not precluded by restrictions & exceptions specified in the constitution; or not immoral, or not contrary to the essential ends of political society.

This principle in its application to Government in general would be admitted as an axiom. And it will be incumbent upon those, who may incline to deny it, to *prove* a distinction; and to shew that a rule which in the general system of things is essential to the preservation of the social order is inapplicable to the United States.

Harold C. Syrett et al., eds., *The Papers of Alexander Hamilton,* 27 vols. (New York: Columbia University Press, 1961–87), 8:97–107, 119–22, 128–30.

The circumstances that the powers of sovereignty are in this country divided between the National and State Governments, does not afford the distinction required. It does not follow from this, that each of the *portions* of powers delegated to the one or to the other is not sovereign *with regard to its proper objects.* It will only *follow* from it, that each has sovereign power as to *certain things,* and not as to *other things.* To deny that the Government of the United States has sovereign power as to its declared purposes & trusts, because its power does not extend to all cases, would be equally to deny, that the State Governments have sovereign power in any case; because their power does not extend to every case. The tenth section of the first article of the constitution exhibits a long list of very important things which they may not do. And thus the United States would furnish the singular spectacle of a *political society* without *sovereignty,* or of a people *governed* without *government.*

If it would be necessary to bring proof to a proposition so clear as that which affirms that the powers of the fœderal government, *as to its objects,* are sovereign, there is a clause of its constitution which would be decisive. It is that which declares, that the constitution and the laws of the United States made in pursuance of it, and all treaties made or which shall be made under their authority shall be the supreme law of the land. The power which can create the *Supreme law* of the land, in any case, is doubtless sovereign *as to such case.*

This general & indisputable principle puts at once an end to the *abstract* question — Whether the United States have power to *erect a corporation?* that is to say, to give a *legal* or *artificial capacity* to one or more persons, distinct from the natural. For it is unquestionably incident to *sovereign power* to erect corporations, and consequently to *that* of the United States, in *relation to the objects* intrusted to the management of the government. The difference is this — where the authority of the government is general, it can create corporations in *all cases;* where it is confined to certain branches of legislation, it can create corporations only in those cases. . . .

It is not denied, that there are *implied,* as well as *express* powers, and that the former are as effectually delegated as the latter. And for the sake of accuracy it shall be mentioned, that there is another class of powers, which may be properly denominated *resulting* powers. It will not be doubted that if the United States should make a conquest of any of the territories of its neighbours, they would possess sovereign jurisdiction over the conquered territory. This would rather be a result from the whole mass of the powers of the government & from the nature of political society, than a consequence of either of the powers specially enumerated.

But be this as it may, it furnishes a striking illustration of the general doctrine contended for. It shews an extensive case, in which a power of erecting corporations is either implied in, or would result from some or all of the powers, vested in the National Government. The jurisdiction acquired over such conquered territory would certainly be competent to every species of legislation.

To return — It is conceded, that implied powers are to be considered as delegated equally with express ones.

Then it follows, that as a power of erecting a corporation may as well be *implied* as any other thing; it may as well be employed as an *instrument* or *mean* of carrying into execution any of the specified powers, as any other instrument or mean whatever. The only question must be, in this as in every other case, whether the mean to be employed, or in this instance the corporation to be erected, has a natural relation to any of the acknowledged objects or lawful ends of the government. Thus a corporation may not be erected by congress, for superintending the police of the city of Philadelphia because they are not authorised to *regulate* the *police* of that city; but one may be erected in relation to the collection of the taxes, or to the trade with foreign countries, or to the trade between the States, or with the Indian Tribes, because it is the province of the fœderal government to regulate those objects & because it is incident to a general *sovereign* or *legislative power* to *regulate* a thing, to employ all the means which relate to its regulation to the *best & greatest advantage.* . . .

To this mode of reasoning respecting the right of employing all the means requisite to the execution of the specified powers of the Government, it is objected that none but *necessary* & proper means are to be employed, & the Secretary of State maintains, that no means are to be considered as *necessary,* but those without which the grant of the power would be *nugatory.* Nay so far does he go in his restrictive interpretation of the word, as even to make the case of *necessity* which shall warrant the constitutional exercise of the power to depend on *casual* & *temporary* circumstances, an idea which alone refutes the construction. The *expediency* of exercising a particular power, at a particular time, must indeed depend on *circumstances;* but the constitutional right of exercising it must be uniform & invariable — the same to day, as to morrow.

All the arguments therefore against the constitutionality of the bill derived from the accidental existence of certain State-banks: institutions which *happen* to exist to day, & for ought that concerns the government of the United States, may disappear to morrow, must not only be rejected as fallacious, but must be viewed as demonstrative, that there is a *radical* source of error in the reasoning.

It is essential to the being of the National government, that so erroneous a conception of the meaning of the word *necessary,* should be exploded.

It is certain, that neither the grammatical, nor popular sense of the term requires that construction. According to both, *necessary* often means no more than *needful, requisite, incidental, useful,* or *conducive to.* It is a common mode of expression to say, that it is *necessary* for a government or a person to do this or that thing, when nothing more is intended or understood, than that the interests of the government or person require, or will be promoted, by the doing of this or that thing. The imagination can be at no loss for exemplifications of the use of the word in this sense.

And it is the true one in which it is to be understood as used in the constitution. The whole turn of the clause containing it, indicates, that it was the intent of the convention, by that clause to give a liberal latitude to the exercise of the specified powers. The expressions have peculiar comprehensiveness. They are — "to make *all laws,* necessary & proper for *carrying into execution* the foregoing powers & all *other powers* vested by the constitution in the *government* of the United States, or in any *department* or *officer* thereof." To understand the word as the Secretary of State does, would be to depart from its obvious & popular sense, and to give it a *restrictive* operation; an idea never before entertained. It would be to give it the same force as if the word *absolutely* or *indispensibly* had been prefixed to it.

Such a construction would beget endless uncertainty & embarassment. The cases must be palpable & extreme in which it could be pronounced with certainty, that a measure was absolutely necessary, or one without which the exercise of a given power would be nugatory. There are few measures of any government, which would stand so severe a test. To insist upon it, would be to make the criterion of the exercise of any implied power a *case of extreme necessity;* which is rather a rule to justify the overleaping of the bounds of constitutional authority, than to govern the ordinary exercise of it.

It may be truly said of every government, as well as of that of the United States, that it has only a right, to pass such laws as are necessary & proper to accomplish the objects intrusted to it. For no government has a right to do *merely what it pleases.* Hence by a process of reasoning similar to that of the Secretary of State, it might be proved, that neither of the State governments has a right to incorporate a bank. It might be shewn, that all the public business of the State, could be performed without a bank, and inferring thence that it was unnecessary it might be argued that it could not be done, because it is against the rule which has been just mentioned. A like mode of reasoning would prove, that there was no power to incorporate the Inhabitants of a town, with a view to a more perfect police: For it is certain, that an incorporation may be dispensed with, though it is better to have one. It is to be remembered, that there is no *express* power in any State constitution to erect corporations.

The *degree* in which a measure is necessary, can never be a test of the *legal* right to adopt it. That must ever be a matter of opinion; and can only be a test of expediency. The *relation* between the *measure* and the *end,* between the *nature* of *the mean* employed towards the execution of a power and the object of that power, must be the criterion of constitutionality not the more or less of *necessity* or *utility.*

The practice of the government is against the rule of construction advocated by the Secretary of State. Of this the act concerning light houses, beacons, buoys & public piers, is a decisive example. This doubtless must be referred to the power of regulating trade, and is fairly relative to it. But it cannot be affirmed, that the exercise of that power, in this instance, was strictly necessary; or that the power itself would be *nugatory* without that of regulating establishments of this nature.

This restrictive interpretation of the word *necessary* is also contrary to this sound maxim of construction namely, that the powers contained in a constitution of government, especially those which concern the general administration of the affairs of a country, its finances, trade, defence &c ought to be construed liberally, in advancement of the public good. This rule does not depend on the particular form of a government or on the particular demarkation of the boundaries of its powers, but on the nature and objects of government itself. The means by which national exigencies are to be provided for, national inconveniencies obviated, national prosperity promoted, are of such infinite variety, extent and complexity, that there must, of necessity, be great latitude of discretion in the selection & application of those means. Hence consequently, the necessity & propriety of exercising the authorities intrusted to a government on principles of liberal construction. . . .

But the doctrine which is contended for is not chargeable with the consequence imputed to it. It does not affirm that the National government is sovereign in all respects, but that it is sovereign to a certain extent: that is, to the extent of the objects of its specified powers.

It leaves therefore a criterion of what is constitutional, and of what is not so. This criterion is the *end* to which the measure relates as a *mean*. If the end be clearly comprehended within any of the specified powers, & if the measure have an obvious relation to that end, and is not forbidden by any particular provision of the constitution — it may safely be deemed to come within the compass of the national authority. There is also this further criterion which may materially assist the decision. Does the proposed measure abridge a preexisting right of any State, or of any individual? If it does not, there is a strong presumption in favour of its constitutionality; & slighter relations to any declared object of the constitution may be permitted to turn the scale. . . .

It is presumed to have been satisfactorily shewn in the course of the preceding observations

1. That the power of the government, *as to* the objects intrusted to its management, is in its nature sovereign.
2. That the right of erecting corporations is one, inherent in & inseparable from the idea of sovereign power.
3. That the position, that the government of the United States can

exercise no power but such as is delegated to it by its constitution, does not militate against this principle.

4. That the word *necessary* in the general clause can have no *restrictive* operation, derogating from the force of this principle, indeed, that the degree in which a measure is, or is not necessary, cannot be a *test* of *constitutional* right, but of expediency only.

5. That the power to erect corporations is not to be considered, as an *independent & substantive* power but as an *incidental & auxiliary* one; and was therefore more properly left to implication, than expressly granted.

6. that the principle in question does not extend the power of the government beyond the prescribed limits, because it only affirms a power to *incorporate* for *purposes within the sphere of the specified powers.*

And lastly that the right to exercise such a power, in certain cases, is unequivocally granted in the most *positive & comprehensive* terms.

To all which it only remains to be added that such a power has actually been exercised in two very eminent instances: namely in the erection of two governments, One, northwest of the river Ohio, and the other south west — *the last, independent of any antecedent compact.*

And there results a full & complete demonstration, that the Secretary of State & Attorney General are mistaken, when they deny generally the power of the National government to erect corporations.

It shall now be endeavoured to be shewn that there is a power to erect one of the kind proposed by the bill. This will be done, by tracing a natural & obvious relation between the institution of a bank, and the objects of several of the enumerated powers of the government; and by shewing that, *politically* speaking, it is necessary to the effectual execution of one or more of those powers. In the course of this investigation, various instances will be stated, by way of illustration, of a right to erect corporations under those powers.

Some preliminary observations maybe proper.

The proposed bank is to consist of an association of persons for the purpose of creating a joint capital to be employed, chiefly and essentially, in loans. So far the object is not only lawful, but it is the mere exercise of a right, which the law allows to every individual. The bank of New York which is not incorporated, is an example of such an association. The bill proposes in addition, that the government shall become a joint proprietor in this undertaking, and that it shall permit the bills of the company payable on demand to be receivable in its revenues & stipulates that it shall not grant privileges similar to those which are to be allowed to this company, to any others. All this is incontrovertibly within the compass of the discretion of the government. The only question is, whether it has a right to incorporate this company, in order to enable it the more effectually to accomplish *ends,* which are in themselves lawful.

To establish such a right, it remains to shew the relation of such an institution to one or more of the specified powers of the government.

Accordingly it is affirmed, that it has a relation more or less direct to the power of collecting taxes; to that of borrowing money; to that of regulating trade between the states; and to those of raising, supporting & maintaining fleets & armies. To the two former, the relation may be said to be *immediate.*

And, in the last place, it will be argued, that it is, *clearly,* within the provision which authorises the making of all *needful* rules & *regulations* concerning the *property* of the United States, as the same has been practiced upon by the Government. . . .

The institution of a bank has also a natural relation to the regulation of trade between the States: in so far as it is conducive to the creation of a convenient medium of *exchange* between them, and to the keeping up a full circulation by preventing the frequent displacement of the metals in reciprocal remittances. Money is the very hinge on which commerce turns. And this does not mean merely gold & silver, many other things have served the purpose with different degrees of utility. Paper has been extensively employed. . . .

There is an observation of the secretary of state . . . which may require notice in this place. Congress, says he, are not to lay taxes *ad libitum for any purpose they please,* but only to pay the debts, or provide for the *welfare* of the Union. Certainly no inference can be drawn from this against the power of applying their money for the institution of a bank. It is true, that they cannot without breach of trust, lay taxes for any other purpose than the general welfare but so neither can any other government. The welfare of the community is the only legitimate end for which money can be raised on the community. Congress can be considered as under only one restriction, which does not apply to other governments — They cannot rightfully apply the money they raise to any purpose *merely* or purely local. But with this exception they have as large a discretion in relation to the *application* of money as any legislature whatever. The constitutional *test* of a right application must always be whether it be for a purpose of *general* or *local* nature. If the former, there can be no want of constitutional power. The quality of the object, as how far it will really promote or not the welfare of the union, must be matter of conscientious discretion. And the arguments for or against a measure in this light, must be arguments concerning expediency or inexpediency, not constitutional right. Whatever relates to the general order of the finances, to the general interests of trade &c being general objects are constitutional ones for *the application* of *money.*

A Bank then whose bills are to circulate in all the revenues of the country, is *evidently* a general object, and for that very reason a constitutional one as far as regards the appropriation of money to it. Whether it will really be a beneficial one, or not, is worthy of careful examination, but is no more a constitutional point, in the particular referred to; than the question whether the western lands shall be sold for twenty or thirty cents ℔ acre.

A hope is entertained, that it has by this time been made to appear, to the satisfaction of the President, that a bank has a natural relation to the power of collecting taxes; to that of borrowing money; to that of regulating trade; to that of providing for the common defence: and that as the bill under consideration contemplates the government in the light of a joint proprietor of the stock of the bank, it brings the case within the provision of the clause of the constitution which immediately respects the property of the United States.

Under a conviction that such a relation subsists, the Secretary of the Treasury, with all deference conceives, that it will result as a necessary consequence from the position, that all the specified powers of the government are sovereign as to the proper objects; that the incorporation of a bank is a constitutional measure, and that the objections taken to the bill, in this respect, are ill founded. . . .

While waiting for Hamilton's opinion, Washington consulted with James Madison, who had opposed the bank bill in Congress. The president also asked Madison to draft a veto message should he decide against signing the bill.[9]

Hamilton had less than a week to prepare his opinion, and when he hurriedly sent his lengthy paper to the president on February 23, 1791, he remarked that it had "occupied him the greatest part of last night." Years later, his wife vividly recalled staying up all night, copying his writing. After receiving Hamilton's lengthy opinion, the president was pressed to make his decision before the act, if not vetoed, would become law without his signature. But Hamilton's brilliant treatise was persuasive, and Washington signed the bill to incorporate the bank on February 25, the last day before the act would become law without his signature. A week later, on March 3, 1791, the First Congress adjourned.[10]

[9] Madison, draft of veto of bank bill, Feb. 21, 1791, in Hutchinson et al., eds., *Madison Papers,* 13:395–96; Ralph Ketcham, *James Madison: A Biography* (New York: Macmillan, 1971), p. 321.

[10] Hamilton to Washington, Feb. 23, 1791, in Syrett et al., eds., *Hamilton Papers,* 8:62; Broadus Mitchell, *Alexander Hamilton: The National Adventure, 1788–1804* (New York: Macmillan, 1962), p. 99.

Figure 4. *Bank of the United States, on Third Street, Philadelphia.*
Drawn, engraved, and published by William Birch & Son. Sold by R. Campbell & Co., No. 30 Chestnut Street, Philadelphia, 1799.
Library of Congress, Prints and Photographs Division.

On July 4, 1791, the stock of the Bank of the United States went on sale in Philadelphia and was oversubscribed on the same day.[11] Success would follow quickly, and before the decade was over, the Bank of the United States would be housed in one of the most impressive buildings in Philadelphia (Figure 4).

Jefferson's opposition to the Bank of the United States did not end when it was chartered. In a private letter written in 1796 that became public a year later, Jefferson denounced the bank as "a contrivance invented for the purposes of corruption, and for assimilating us in all things to the rotten as well as the sound parts of the British model."[12]

---

[11] Syrett et al., eds., *Hamilton Papers,* 9:114.
[12] Jefferson to Philip Mazzei, Apr. 24, 1796, in Paul L. Ford, ed., *The Works of Thomas Jefferson,* Federal Edition, 12 vols. (New York: G. P. Putnam's Sons, 1904), 8:237–40.

Because Jefferson and Hamilton wrote their opinions to advise the president privately, Washington did not make them public. He did, however, retain the documents among his papers, and after Washington's death, Chief Justice John Marshall had access to those papers in writing his biography of Washington. Marshall included excerpts from both Jefferson's and Hamilton's opinions in an eight-page note appended to the final volume of that biography, published in 1807 while Jefferson was president.[13] In 1819, in the decision in the case of *McCulloch v. Maryland,* Chief Justice Marshall, using arguments that Hamilton had made, upheld the constitutionality of the Bank of the United States.

For a time, the developing differences between Hamilton and Jefferson were not widely known, but in the spring of 1791, Jefferson inadvertently appeared in the public press as a dissenter within the administration. He had been loaned a copy of Thomas Paine's *Rights of Man,* as it passed through the hands of several interested readers before being reprinted in Philadelphia. In 1776, Paine had written *Common Sense,* advocating American independence. Paine's 1791 pamphlet defended republican government and the French Revolution at a time when the revolutionary events in France struck alarm in much of Europe. After Jefferson received word to send the pamphlet to the printer, he accompanied it with a brief note expressing his pleasure that it was to be reprinted. When the work was published, most of Jefferson's note appeared in a foreword announcing, "The following Extract from a note accompanying a copy of this Pamphlet for republication, is so respectable a testimony of its value, that the Printer hopes the distinguished writer will excuse its present appearance." After thus connecting Jefferson with the publication of Paine's work, printer Samuel Harrison Smith quoted the secretary of state as writing,

> I am extremely pleased to find it will be reprinted here, and that something is at length to be publicly said against the political heresies which had sprung up among us.
> I have no doubt our citizens will *rally* a second time round the *standard* of COMMON SENSE.[14]

Jefferson had indeed written these words, but he had not intended them for publication. Because he approved of Paine's pamphlet, he could

---

[13]John Marshall, *The Life of George Washington,* 5 vols. (Philadelphia: C. P. Wayne, 1804–7), pp. 3–11 of appended notes to vol. 5.

[14]Boyd, Cullen, and Catanzariti, eds., *Jefferson Papers,* 20:271–73, 290, following p. 384.

not now disavow commending it. The embarrassment was greater because it was widely assumed that "the political heresies" referred to by Jefferson were writings signed "Davila"—commonly recognized as written by Vice President John Adams. "I tell the writer freely that he is a heretic," Jefferson confided to James Madison, "but certainly never meant to step into a public newspaper with that in my mouth."[15]

Later in the year, in a conversation with Jefferson, Hamilton strongly condemned John Adams's "Davila" writings. Afterward, Jefferson made the following detailed note on their conversation (Figure 5), recording Hamilton as making the following remarks.

[15] Jefferson to Madison, May 9, 1791, ibid., 293.

THOMAS JEFFERSON

Notes of a Conversation between Alexander Hamilton and Thomas Jefferson

August 13, 1791

"I own it is my own opinion, tho' I do not publish it in Dan and Bersheba,[16] that the present government is not that which will answer the ends of society, by giving stability and protection to it's rights, and that it will probably be found expedient to go into the British form. However, since we have undertaken the experiment, I am for giving it a fair course, whatever my expectations may be. The success indeed so far is greater than I had expected, and therefore at present success seems more possible than it had done heretofore, and there are still other and other stages of improvement which, if the present does not succeed, may be tried and ought to be tried before we give up the republican form altogether, for that mind must be really depraved which would not prefer the equality of political rights which is the foundation of pure republicanism, if it can be obtained consistently with order. Therefore whoever by his writings disturbs the present order of things, is really blameable, however pure his intentions may be, and he was sure Mr. Adams's were pure."— This is the substance of a declaration made in much more lengthy terms, and which seemed to be

[16] An expression for the whole of Palestine, Dan being the northern-most town in biblical Palestine and Bersheba, the southern-most town.

Julian P. Boyd, Charles T. Cullen, and John Catanzariti, eds., *The Papers of Thomas Jefferson,* 27 vols. to date (Princeton: Princeton University Press, 1950–), 22:38–39.

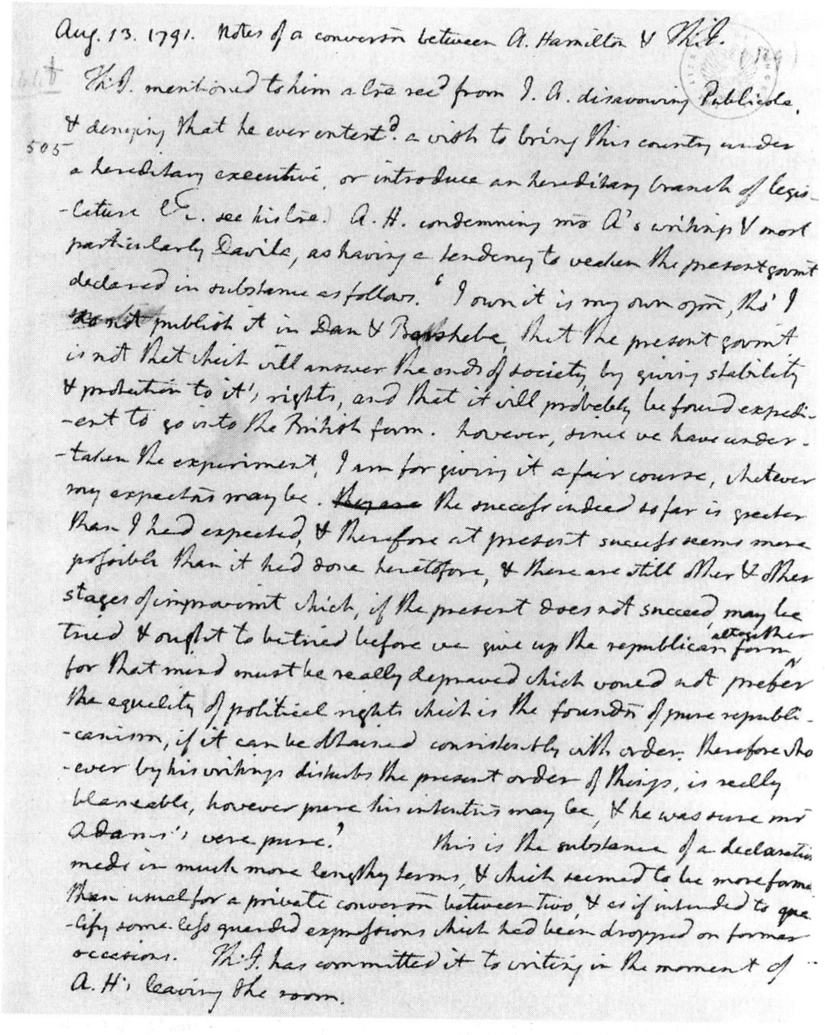

Figure 5. *Notes of a Conversation between Alexander Hamilton and Thomas Jefferson, August 13, 1791.*

The notes were recorded by Jefferson immediately after Hamilton left the room. Thomas Jefferson Papers, Library of Congress, Manuscript Division.

more formal than usual for a conversation between two,
to qualify some less guarded expressions which had beer.
mer occasions.— Th:J has committed it to writing in the n
leaving the room.

A few months after Jefferson recorded this conversation, the divergence of views of the two statesmen would be further displayed when Hamilton submitted his *Report on Manufactures* to the opening session of the Second Congress. He had written four drafts of the important report before sending the final version to the House of Representatives on December 5, 1791. It was the longest and most impressive of the Treasury secretary's papers, but unlike his reports to the First Congress, this treatise would not lead to the passage of legislation to implement the proposals.

Jefferson did not share Hamilton's view of the need and importance of encouraging manufacturing in the United States. In his *Notes on the State of Virginia,* printed in 1785, the Virginia native had praised the virtues of an agrarian society and had argued against the promotion of manufacturing in the United States. He had noted that the political economists of Europe reasoned that every state should endeavor to manufacture for itself, but that this principle had been transferred to America without calculating the difference of circumstances. Lands in Europe were either cultivated or "locked up against the cultivator," and manufacturing was resorted to in order to support the surplus of people. On the other hand, in America there was "an immensity of land courting the industry of the husbandman." Jefferson continued,

> Those who labour in the earth are the chosen people of God, if ever he had a chosen people, whose breasts he has made his peculiar deposit for substantial and genuine virtue. . . . While we have land to labour then, let us never wish to see our citizens occupied at a work-bench, or twirling a distaff. Carpenters, masons, smiths, are wanting in husbandry: but, for the general operations of manufacture, let our work-shops remain in Europe. . . . The mobs of great cities add just so much to the support of pure government, as sores do to the strength of the human body. It is the manners and spirit of a people which preserve a republic in vigour.[17]

---

[17] Thomas Jefferson, *Notes on the State of Virginia,* ed. William Peden (Chapel Hill: University of North Carolina Press, 1954), pp. 164–65. A distaff was a staff for holding flax or wool in spinning.

amilton's *Report on Manufactures* displayed him at his best as an economic planner, and it also revealed fundamental differences with Jefferson, who believed that the tillers of the soil were the chosen people of God. Hamilton sought to demonstrate that the promotion of manufacturing would make the United States independent of foreign nations for military and other essential supplies. Even more than his defense of the Bank of the United States, Hamilton's *Report on Manufactures* revealed his hopes and plans for an expansion of the American economy well beyond its agrarian base.

The following extract is from the introduction to Hamilton's detailed report, in which he made the case for protective tariffs, the exemption of essential raw materials from import duties, and government subsidies for new industries.

ALEXANDER HAMILTON

Introduction to the Report on Manufactures

December 5, 1791

The Secretary of the Treasury in obedience to the order of ye House of Representatives, of the 15th day of January 1790, has applied his attention, at as early a period as his other duties would permit, to the subject of Manufactures; and particularly to the means of promoting such as will tend to render the United States, independent on foreign nations, for military and other essential supplies. And he there[upon] respectfully submits the following Report.

The expediency of encouraging manufactures in the United States, which was not long since deemed very questionable, appears at this time to be pretty generally admitted. The embarrassments, which have obstructed the progress of our external trade, have led to serious reflections on the necessity of enlarging the sphere of our domestic commerce: the restrictive regulations, which in foreign markets abrige the vent of the increasing surplus of our Agricultural produce, serve to beget an earnest desire, that a more extensive demand for that surplus may be created at home: And the complete success, which has rewarded manufacturing en-

Harold C. Syrett et al., eds., *The Papers of Alexander Hamilton,* 27 vols. (New York: Columbia University Press, 1961–87), 10:230–61.

terprise, in some valuable branches, conspiring with the promising symptoms, which attend some less mature essays, in others, justify a hope, that the obstacles to the growth of this species of industry are less formidable than they were apprehended to be; and that it is not difficult to find, in its further extension; a full indemnification for any external disadvantages, which are or may be experienced, as well as an accession of resources, favourable to national independence and safety. . . .

It ought readily to be conceded, that the cultivation of the earth — as the primary and most certain source of national supply — as the immediate and chief source of subsistence to man — as the principal source of those materials which constitute the nutriment of other kinds of labor — as including a state most favorable to the freedom and independence of the human mind — one, perhaps, most conducive to the multiplication of the human species — has *intrinsically a strong claim to pre-eminence over every other kind of industry.*

But, that it has a title to any thing like an exclusive predilection, in any country, ought to be admitted with great caution. That it is even more productive than every other branch of Industry requires more evidence, than has yet been given in support of the position. That its real interests, precious and important as without the help of exaggeration, they truly are, will be advanced, rather than injured by the due encouragement of manufactures, may, it is believed, be satisfactorily demonstrated. And it is also believed that the expediency of such encouragement in a general view may be shewn to be recommended by the most cogent and persuasive motives of national policy.

It has been maintained, that Agriculture is, not only, the most productive, but the only productive species of industry. The reality of this suggestion in either aspect, has, however, not been verified by any accurate detail of facts and calculations; and the general arguments, which are adduced to prove it, are rather subtil and paradoxical, than solid or convincing. . . .

But without contending for the superior productiveness of Manufacturing Industry, it may conduce to a better judgment of the policy, which ought to be pursued respecting its encouragement, to contemplate the subject, under some additional aspects, tending not only to confirm the idea, that this kind of industry has been improperly represented as unproductive in itself; but [to] evince in addition that the establishment and diffusion of manufactures have the effect of rendering the total mass of useful and productive labor in a community, *greater than it would otherwise be.* In prosecuting this discussion, it may be necessary briefly to resume and review some of the topics, which have been already touched.

To affirm, that the labour of the Manufacturer is unproductive, because he consumes as much of the produce of land, as he adds value to the raw materials which he manufactures, is not better founded, than it would be to affirm, that the labour of the farmer, which furnishes materials to the manufacturer, is unproductive, *because he consumes an equal value of manufactured articles.* Each furnishes a certain portion of the produce of his labor to the other, and each destroys a correspondent portion of the produce of the labour of the other. In the mean time, the maintenance of two Citizens, instead of one, is going on; the State has two members instead of one; and they together consume twice the value of what is produced from the land.

If instead of a farmer and artificer, there were a farmer only, he would be under the necessity of devoting a part of his labour to the fabrication of cloathing and other articles, which he would procure of the artificer, in the case of there being such a person; and of course he would be able to devote less labor to the cultivation of his farm; and would draw from it a proportionably less product. The whole quantity of production, in this state of things, in provisions, raw materials and manufactures, would certainly not exceed in value the amount of what would be produced in provisions and raw materials only, if there were an artificer as well as a farmer.

Again — if there were both an artificer and a farmer, the latter would be left at liberty to pursue exclusively the cultivation of his farm. A greater quantity of provisions and raw materials would of course be produced — equal at least — as has been already observed, to the whole amount of the provisions, raw materials and manufactures, which would exist on a contrary supposition. The artificer, at the same time would be going on in the production of manufactured commodities; to an amount sufficient not only to repay the farmer, in those commodities, for the provisions and materials which were procured from him, but to furnish the Artificer himself with a supply of similar commodities for his own use. Thus, then, there would be two quantities or values in existence, instead of one; and the revenue and consumption would be double in one case, what it would be in the other. . . .

It is now proper to proceed a step further, and to enumerate the principal circumstances, from which it may be inferred — That manufacturing establishments not only occasion a possitive augmentation of the Produce and Revenue of the Society, but that they contribute essentially to rendering them greater than they could possibly be, without such establishments. These circumstances are —

1. The division of Labour.
2. An extension of the use of Machinery.
3. Additional employment to classes of the community not ordinarily engaged in the business.
4. The promoting of emigration from foreign Countries.
5. The furnishing greater scope for the diversity of talents and dispositions which discriminate men from each other.
6. The affording a more ample and various field for enterprize.
7. The creating in some instances a new, and securing in all, a more certain and steady demand for the surplus produce of the soil.

Each of these circumstances has a considerable influence upon the total mass of industrious effort in a community. Together, they add to it a degree of energy and effect, which are not easily conceived. Some comments upon each of them, in the order in which they have been stated, may serve to explain their importance.

I. As to the Division of Labour.

It has justly been observed, that there is scarcely any thing of greater moment in the economy of a nation, than the proper division of labour. The separation of occupations causes each to be carried to a much greater perfection, than it could possibly acquire, if they were blended. This arises principally from three circumstances.

1st — The greater skill and dexterity naturally resulting from a constant and undivided application to a single object. It is evident, that these properties must increase, in proportion to the separation and simplification of objects and the steadiness of the attention devoted to each; and must be less, in proportion to the complication of objects, and the number among which the attention is distracted.

2nd. The economy of time — by avoiding the loss of it, incident to a frequent transition from one operation to another of a different nature. This depends on various circumstances — the transition itself — the orderly disposition of the impliments, machines and materials employed in the operation to be relinquished — the preparatory steps to the commencement of a new one — the interruption of the impulse, which the mind of the workman acquires, from being engaged in a particular operation — the distractions hesitations and reluctances, which attend the passage from one kind of business to another.

3rd. An extension of the use of Machinery. A man occupied on a single object will have it more in his power, and will be more naturally led to exert his imagination in devising methods to facilitate and abrige labour, than if he were perplexed by a variety of independent and dissimilar operations. Besides this, the fabrication of Machines, in numerous instances, becoming itself a distinct trade, the Artist who follows it, has all the advantages which have been enumerated, for improvement in his particular art; and in both ways the invention and application of machinery are extended.

And from these causes united, the mere separation of the occupation of the cultivator, from that of the Artificer, has the effect of augmenting the *productive powers* of labour, and with them, the total mass of the produce or revenue of a Country. In this single view of the subject, therefore, the utility of Artificers or Manufacturers, towards promoting an increase of productive industry, is apparent.

II. As to an extension of the use of Machinery a point which though partly anticipated requires to be placed in one or two additional lights.

The employment of Machinery forms an item of great importance in the general mass of national industry. 'Tis an artificial force brought in aid of the natural force of man; and, to all the purposes of labour, is an increase of hands; an accession of strength, *unincumbered too by the expense of maintaining the laborer.* May it not therefore be fairly inferred, that those occupations, which give greatest scope to the use of this auxiliary, contribute most to the general Stock of industrious effort, and, in consequence, to the general product of industry?

It shall be taken for granted, and the truth of the position referred to observation, that manufacturing pursuits are susceptible in a greater degree of the application of machinery, than those of Agriculture. If so all the difference is lost to a community, which, instead of manufacturing for itself, procures the fabrics requisite to its supply from other Countries. The substitution of foreign for domestic manufactures is a transfer to foreign nations of the advantages accruing from the employment of Machinery, in the modes in which it is capable of being employed, with most utility and to the greatest extent.

The Cotton Mill invented in England, within the last twenty years, is a signal illustration of the general proposition, which has been just advanced. In consequence of it, all the different processes for spinning Cotton are performed by means of Machines, which are put in motion by water, and attended chiefly by women and Children; [and by a smaller] number of [persons, in the whole, than are] requisite in the ordinary mode of spinning. And it is an advantage of great moment that the operations of this mill continue with convenience, during the night, as well as through the day. The prodigious affect of such a Machine is easily conceived. To this invention is to be attributed essentially the immense progress, which has been so suddenly made in Great Britain in the various fabrics of Cotton.

III. As to the additional employment of classes of the community, not ordinarily engaged in the particular business.

This is not among the least valuable of the means, by which manufacturing institutions contribute to augment the general stock of industry and production. In places where those institutions prevail, besides the persons regularly engaged in them, they afford occasional and extra employment to industrious individuals and families, who are willing to devote the leisure resulting from the intermissions of their ordinary pursuits to collateral labours, as a resource of multiplying their acquisitions or [their] enjoyments. The husbandman himself experiences a new source of profit and support from the encreased industry of his wife and daughters; invited and stimulated by the demands of the neighboring manufactories.

Besides this advantage of occasional employment to classes having different occupations, there is another of a nature allied to it [and] of a similar tendency. This is — the employment of persons who would otherwise be idle (and in many cases a burthen on the community), either from the byass of temper, habit, infirmity of body, or some other cause, indisposing, or disqualifying them for the toils of the Country. It is worthy of particular remark, that, in general, women and Children are rendered more useful and the latter more early useful by manufacturing establishments, than they would otherwise be. Of the number of persons employed in the Cotton Manufactories of Great Britain, it is computed that 4/7 nearly are women and children; of whom the greatest proportion are children and many of them of a very tender age.

And thus it appears to be one of the attributes of manufactures, and one of no small consequence, to give occasion to the exertion of a greater quantity of Industry, even by the *same number* of persons, where they happen to prevail, than would exist, if there were no such establishments.

IV. As to the promoting of emigration from foreign Countries.

Men reluctantly quit one course of occupation and livelihood for another, unless invited to it by very apparent and proximate advantages. Many, who would go from one country to another, if they had a prospect of continuing with more benefit the callings, to which they have been educated, will often not be tempted to change their situation, by the hope of doing better, in some other way. Manufacturers, who listening to the powerful invitations of a better price for their fabrics, or their labour, of greater cheapness of provisions and raw materials, of an exemption from the chief part of the taxes burthens and restraints, which they endure in the old world, of greater personal independence and consequence, under the operation of a more equal government, and of what is far more precious than mere religious toleration — a perfect equality of religious privileges; would probably flock from Europe to the United States to pursue their own trades or professions, if they were once made sensible of the advantages they would enjoy, and were inspired with an assurance of encouragement and employment, will, with difficulty, be induced to transplant themselves, with a view to becoming Cultivators of Land.

If it be true then, that it is the interest of the United States to open every possible [avenue to] emigration from abroad, it affords a weighty argument for the encouragement of manufactures; which for the reasons just assigned, will have the strongest tendency to multiply the inducements to it.

Here is perceived an important resource, not only for extending the population, and with it the useful and productive labour of the country, but likewise for the prosecution of manufactures, without deducting from the number of hands, which might otherwise be drawn to tillage; and even for the indemnification of Agriculture for such as might happen to be diverted from it. Many, whom Manufacturing views would induce to emigrate, would afterwards yield to the temptations, which the particular situation of this Country holds out to Agricultural pursuits. And while Agriculture would in other respects derive many signal and unmingled advantages, from the growth of manufactures, it is a problem whether it would gain or lose, as to the article of the number of persons employed in carrying it on.

V. As to the furnishing greater scope for the diversity of talents and dispositions, which discriminate men from each other.

This is a much more powerful mean of augmenting the fund of national Industry than may at first sight appear. It is a just observation, that minds of the strongest and most active powers for their proper objects fall below mediocrity and labour without effect, if confined to uncongenial pursuits. And it is thence to be inferred, that the results of human exertion may be immensely increased by diversifying its objects. When all the different kinds of industry obtain in a community, each individual can find his proper element, and can call into activity the whole vigour of his nature. And the community is benefitted by the services of its respective members, in the manner, in which each can serve it with most effect.

If there be anything in a remark often to be met with — namely that there is, in the genius of the people of this country, a peculiar aptitude for mechanic improvements, it would operate as a forcible reason for giving opportunities to the exercise of that species of talent, by the propagation of manufactures.

VI. As to the affording a more ample and various field for enterprise.

This also is of greater consequence in the general scale of national exertion, than might perhaps on a superficial view be supposed, and has effects not altogether dissimilar from those of the circumstance last noticed. To cherish and stimulate the activity of the human mind, by multiplying the objects of enterprise, is not among the least considerable of the expedients, by which the wealth of a nation may be promoted. Even things in themselves not positively advantageous, sometimes become so, by their tendency to provoke exertion. Every new scene, which is opened to the busy nature of man to rouse and exert itself, is the addition of a new energy to the general stock of effort.

The spirit of enterprise, useful and prolific as it is, must necessarily be contracted or expanded in proportion to the simplicity or variety of the occupations and productions, which are to be found in a Society. It must be less in a nation of mere cultivators, than in a nation of cultivators and merchants; less in a nation of cultivators and merchants, than in a nation of cultivators, artificers and merchants.

VII. As to the creating, in some instances, a new, and securing in all a more certain and steady demand, for the surplus produce of the soil.

This is among the most important of the circumstances which have been indicated. It is a principal mean, by which the establishment of manufactures contributes to an augmentation of the produce or revenue of a country, and has an immediate and direct relation to the prosperity of Agriculture. . . .

Considering how fast and how much the progress of new settlements in the United States must increase the surplus produce of the soil, and weighing seriously the tendency of the system, which prevails among most of the commercial nations of Europe; whatever dependence may be placed on the force of natural circumstances to counteract the effects of an artificial policy; there appear strong reasons to regard the foreign demand for that surplus as too uncertain a reliance, and to desire a substitute for it, in an extensive domestic market.

To secure such a market, there is no other expedient, than to promote manufacturing establishments. Manufacturers who constitute the most numerous class, after the Cultivators of land, are for that reason the principal consumers of the surplus of their labour. . . .

The foregoing considerations seem sufficient to establish, as general propositions, That it is the interest of nations to diversify the industrious pursuits of the individuals, who compose them — That the establishment of manufactures is calculated not only to increase the general stock of useful and productive labour; but even to improve the state of Agriculture in particular; certainly to advance the interests of those who are engaged in it. . . .

In response to Hamilton's proposal to provide government bounties to encourage manufacturing, Jefferson argued that the only power of Congress to do so was that of levying heavy import duties. In a memorandum replying to Hamilton's *Report on Manufactures,* Jefferson opined that household manufactures were to be encouraged but public manufacturing enterprises were not. Few instances of the latter had been successful, he thought, and perhaps none of them without burdening the public. "Bounties have in some instances been a successful instrument for the introduction of new and useful manufactures," he admitted. "But the use of them has been found almost inseparable from abuse." Furthermore, he insisted that the power to provide bounties had not been delegated by the Constitution to the general government. "It remains with the state governments whose local information renders them competent judges of the particular arts and manufactures for which circumstances have matured them."[18]

Years after Hamilton's death, the War of 1812 modified Jefferson's views on manufactures. He took pride in the spread of household manufactures during the war and also welcomed the manufacturing establishments rising in the cities. Indeed, he even acknowledged that "nothing is more certain than that, come peace when it will, we shall never again go to England for a shilling where we have gone for a dollar's

---

[18]Jefferson, notes [Feb. 1792], in Boyd, Cullen, and Catanzariti, eds., *Jefferson Papers,* 23:172–73.

worth."[19] He now approved of commercial capital going into manufacturing; after the war, he supported the tariff of 1816 to protect infant industries. When he learned his earlier views on manufactures were being quoted from his *Notes on Virginia,* Jefferson protested their use to promote dependence on England for manufactures. "There was a time when I might have been so quoted with more candor," he admitted, "but within the thirty years which have since elapsed, how are circumstances changed!"[20] Had he lived, Hamilton would have been amazed to hear Jefferson admit,

> We have experienced what we did not then believe, that there exists both profligacy and power enough to exclude us from the field of interchange with other nations: that to be independent for the comforts of life we must fabricate them ourselves. We must now place the manufacturer by the side of the agriculturist. . . . Experience has taught me that manufactures are now as necessary to our independence as to our comfort.[21]

[19] Jefferson to Thaddeus Kosciusko, June 28, 1812, in Ford, ed., *Jefferson Works,* 11:261.
[20] Jefferson to Benjamin Austin, Jan. 9, 1816, ibid., p. 328.
[21] Ibid., p. 504.

4

Conflict in Washington's Cabinet

When Alexander Hamilton took office as secretary of the Treasury and Thomas Jefferson assumed the office of secretary of state in President George Washington's new administration, there were no national political parties in the United States. The Federalist and Anti-Federalist divisions that had contested the ratification of the Constitution of the United States had not evolved into political parties. In the opening session of the First Congress in 1789, there were no clear partisan alignments. By the second session of that Congress, however, divisions were beginning to coalesce into partisan blocks of Republicans and Federalists. In these emerging political parties, Jefferson and Hamilton played major roles.

The widening differences between Jefferson and Hamilton were sharply revealed in a series of letters written during the spring, summer, and fall of 1792. These letters were exchanged between Jefferson and Washington, between Hamilton and Washington, and between Hamilton and a political confidant, Edward Carrington.

With expanding political polarization and the mounting controversy widely exposed in the Philadelphia press, President Washington began to contemplate retiring from office at the end of his four-year term. As time passed, Jefferson became increasingly concerned about the direction of national affairs. Along with James Madison, he helped Philip Freneau establish the *National Gazette* in Philadelphia to counteract the influence of John Fenno's *Gazette of the United States,* which enjoyed the considerable printing business of the Treasury Department. Under various pseudonyms, Hamilton contributed partisan pieces to Fenno's newspaper. Meanwhile, Jefferson employed Freneau as a part-time translating clerk in the State Department. Jefferson avowed that he "never did by myself or any other, directly or indirectly, write, dictate or procure any one sentence" to be published in Freneau's newspaper, but he did encourage others to contribute to the paper.[1]

Writing to President Washington in late May 1792, Jefferson expressed concern about Hamilton's financial policies, the mounting public debt, and a "corrupt squadron" in Congress seeking to override the limits imposed by the Constitution, and he expressed a general anxiety about the future of the Union. He appealed to Washington to stand for reelection to hold the Union together. In a systematic statement of his opposition to Hamilton's policies, Jefferson expressed his fear that monarchical Federalists sought to use the new government as a stepping-stone to monarchy, and he professed his alignment with "the republican party, who wish to preserve the government in it's present form."

[1]Noble E. Cunningham Jr., *In Pursuit of Reason: The Life of Thomas Jefferson* (Baton Rouge: Louisiana State University Press, 1987), pp. 169–71.

THOMAS JEFFERSON

Letter to George Washington

May 23, 1792

Dear Sir: PHILADELPHIA MAY. 23. 1792.
I have determined to make the subject of a letter, what, for some time past, has been a subject of inquietude to my mind without having found a good occasion of disburthening itself to you in conversation, during the busy scenes which occupied you here. Perhaps too you may be able, in your present situation, or on the road, to give it more time and reflection than you could do here in any moment.

When you first mentioned to me your purpose of retiring from the government, tho' I felt all the magnitude of the event, I was in a considerable degree silent. I knew that, to such a mind as yours, persuasion was idle and impertinent: that before forming your decision, you had weighed all the reasons for and against the measure, had made up your mind on full view of them, and that there could be little hope of changing the result. Pursuing my reflections too I knew we were some day to try to walk alone, and if the essay[2] should be made while you should be alive and

[2]essay: effort.

Julian P. Boyd, Charles T. Cullen, and John Catanzariti, eds., *The Papers of Thomas Jefferson,* 27 vols. to date (Princeton: Princeton University Press, 1950–), 23:535–40.

looking on, we should derive confidence from that circumstance, and resource if it failed. The public mind too was then calm and confident, and therefore in a favorable state for making the experiment. Had no change of circumstances supervened, I should not, with any hope of success, have now ventured to propose to you a change of purpose. But the public mind is no longer so confident and serene; and that from causes in which you are no ways personally mixed. Tho these causes have been hackneyed in the public papers in detail, it may not be amiss, in order to calculate the effect they are capable of producing, to take a view of them in the mass, giving to each the form, real or imaginary, under which they have been presented.

It has been urged then that a public debt, greater than we can possibly pay before other causes of adding new debt to it will occur, has been artificially created, by adding together the whole amount of the debtor and creditor sides of accounts, instead of taking only their balances, which could have been paid off in a short time: That this accumulation of debt has taken for ever out of our power those easy sources of revenue, which, applied to the ordinary necessities and exigencies of government, would have answered them habitually, and covered us from habitual murmurings against taxes and tax-gatherers, reserving extraordinary calls, for those extraordinary occasions which would animate the people to meet them: That though the calls for money have been no greater than we must generally expect, for the same or equivalent exigencies, yet we are already obliged to strain the *impost*[3] till it produces clamour, and will produce evasion, and war on our own citizens to collect it: and even to resort to an *Excise* law, of odious character with the people, partial in it's operation, unproductive unless enforced by arbitrary and vexatious means, and committing the authority of the government, in parts where resistance is most probable, and coercion least practicable. They cite propositions in Congress and suspect other projects on foot still to increase the mass of debt. . . .

That this corrupt squadron, deciding the voice of the legislature, have manifested their dispositions to get rid of the limitations imposed by the constitution on the general legislature, limitations, on the faith of which, the states acceded to that instrument: That the ultimate object of all this is to prepare the way for a change, from the present republican form of government, to that of a monarchy, of which the English constitution is to be the model. That this was contemplated in the [Constitutional] Convention, is no secret, because it's partisans have made none of it. To effect it then was impracticable; but they are still eager after their object, and are predisposing every thing for it's ultimate attainment. So many of them have got into the legislature, that, aided by the corrupt squadron of paper dealers, who are at their devotion, they make a majority in both houses. The

---

[3] *impost:* tax or duty.

republican party, who wish to preserve the government in it's present form, are fewer in number. They are fewer even when joined by the two, three, or half dozen anti-federalists, who, tho they dare not avow it, are still opposed to any general government: but being less so to a republican than a monarchical one, they naturally join those whom they think pursuing the lesser evil.

Of all the mischiefs objected to the system of measures beforementioned, none is so afflicting, and fatal to every honest hope, as the corruption of the legislature. As it was the earliest of these measures it became the instrument for producing the rest, and will be the instrument for producing in future a king, lords and commons, or whatever else those who direct it may chuse. Withdrawn such a distance from the eye of their constituents, and these so dispersed as to be inaccessible to public information, and particularly to that of the conduct of their own representatives, they will form the most corrupt government on earth, if the means of their corruption be not prevented. The only hope of safety hangs now on the numerous representation which is to come forward the ensuing year. Some of the new members will probably be either in principle or interest, with the present majority. But it is expected that the great mass will form an accession to the republican party. They will not be able to undo all which the two preceding legislatures, and especially the first have done. Public faith and right will oppose this. But some parts of the system may be rightfully reformed; a liberation from the rest unremittingly pursued as fast as right will permit, and the door shut in future against similar commitments of the nation. Should the next legislature take this course, it will draw upon them the whole monarchical and paper interest. But the latter I think will not go all lengths with the former, because creditors will never, of their own accord, fly off entirely from their debtors. Therefore this is the alternative least likely to produce convulsion. But should the majority of the new members be still in the same principles with the present and shew that we have nothing to expect but a continuance of the same practices, it is not easy to conjecture what would be the result, nor what means would be resorted to for correction of the evil. True wisdom would direct that they should be temperate and peaceable. But the division of sentiment and interest happens unfortunately to be so geographical, that no mortal can say that what is most wise and temperate would prevail against what is more easy and obvious? I can scarcely contemplate a more incalculable evil than the breaking of the union into two or more parts. Yet when we review the mass which opposed the original coalescence, when we consider that it lay chiefly in the Southern quarter, that the legislature have availed themselves of no occasion of allaying it, but on the contrary whenever Northern and Southern prejudices have come into conflict, the latter have been sacrificed and the former soothed; that the owers of the debt are in the Southern and the holders of it in the Northern division; that the Antifederal champions are now strengthened in argument by the fulfilment of their predictions; that this has been brought about by the Monarchical federalists themselves, who, having been for the new government merely as a stepping stone to monarchy, have themselves adopted the very constructions of the constitution, of which, when advocating it's acceptance before the tribunal of the people, they declared it unsusceptible; that the republican federalists, who espoused the same government for it's intrinsic merits, are disarmed of their weapons, that which they denied as prophecy being now become true history: who can be sure that these things may not proselyte the small number which was wanting to place the majority on the other side? And this is the event at which I tremble, and to prevent which I consider your continuance at the head of affairs as of the last importance. The confidence of the whole union is centered in you. Your being at the helm, will be more than an answer to every argument which can be used to alarm and lead the people in any quarter into violence or secession. North and South will hang together, if they have you to hang on: and, if the first corrective of a numerous representation should fail in it's effect, your presence will give time for trying others not inconsistent with the union and peace of the states.

I am perfectly aware of the oppression under which your present office lays your mind, and of the ardor with which you pant for retirement to domestic life. But there is sometimes an eminence of character on which society have such peculiar claims as to controul the predilection of the individual for a particular walk of happiness, and restrain him to that alone arising from the present and future benedictions of mankind. This seems to be your condition, and the law imposed on you by providence in forming your character, and fashioning the events on which it was to operate: and it is to motives like these, and not to personal anxieties of mine or others who have no right to call on you for sacrifices, that I appeal from your former determination and urge a revisal of it, on the ground of change in the aspect of things. Should an honest majority result from the new and enlarged representation; should those acquiesce whose principles or interests they may controul, your wishes for retirement would be gratified with less danger, as soon as that shall be manifest, without awaiting the completion of the second period of four years. One or two sessions will determine the crisis: and I cannot but hope that you can resolve to add one or two more to the many years you have already sacrificed to the good of mankind.

The fear of suspicion that any selfish motive of continuance in office may enter into this sollicitation on my part obliges me to declare that no such motive exists. It is a thing of mere indifference to the public whether I retain or relinquish my purpose of closing my tour with the first periodical renovation of the government. I know my own measure too well to suppose that my services contribute any thing to the public confidence, or the public utility. Multitudes can fill the office in which you have been pleased to place me, as much to their advantage and satisfaction. *I,* therefore, have no motive to consult but my own inclination, which is bent irresistibly on the tranquil enjoyment of my family, my farm, and my books. I should repose among them it is true, in far greater security, if I were to know that you remained at the watch, and I hope it will be so. To the inducements urged from a view of our domestic affairs, I will add a bare mention, of what indeed need only be mentioned, that weighty motives for your continuance are to be found in our foreign affairs. I think it probable that both the Spanish and English negociations, if not completed before your purpose is known, will be suspended from the moment it is known; and that the latter nation will then use double diligence in fomenting the Indian war. With my wishes for the future, I shall at the same time express my gratitude for the past, at least my portion in it; and beg permission to follow you whether in public or private life with those sentiments of sincere attachment & respect, with which I am unalterably, Dear Sir, Your affectionate friend & humble servant,

TH: JEFFERSON

Jefferson's letter of May 23, 1792, to Washington was sent to Mount Vernon and did not reach the president until after he returned to Philadelphia. It was July before Washington discussed its contents with Jefferson. He then focused on his desire to retire at the end of his four-year term. At the same time, the president suggested that "there were suspicions against a particular party [Hamilton] which had been carried a great deal too far," but he "did not believe that the discontents extended far beyond the seat of government." Having spoken with many people while traveling through Virginia and Maryland, Washington had found "the people contented and happy."[4]

When he returned to Mount Vernon at the end of July, Washington nonetheless drafted the following private letter to Hamilton, listing almost verbatim the arguments from Jefferson's letter while carefully hiding their source.

---

[4] Jefferson, "Notes on a Conversation with George Washington," July 10, 1792, in Julian P. Boyd, Charles T. Cullen, and John Catanzariti, eds., *The Papers of Thomas Jefferson,* 27 vols. to date (Princeton: Princeton University Press, 1950–), 24:210–12.

GEORGE WASHINGTON

Letter to Alexander Hamilton

July 29, 1792

MOUNT VERNON JULY 29TH. 1792.

My dear Sir: (Private & confidential)

. . . On my way home, and since my arrival here, I have endeavoured to learn from sensible & moderate men — known friends to the Government — the sentiments which are entertained of public measures. These all agree that the Country is prosperous & happy; but they seem to be alarmed at that system of policy, and those interpretations of the Constitution with have taken place in Congress.

Others, less friendly perhaps to the Government, and more disposed to arraign the conduct of its Officers . . . go further, & enumerate a variety of matters, wch. as well as I can recollect, may be adduced under the following heads. Viz.

First   That the public debt is greater than we can possibly pay before other causes of adding new debt to it will occur; and that this has been artificially created by adding together the whole amount of the debtor & creditor sides of the accounts, instead of taking only their balances; which could have been paid off in a short time.

2d.   That this accumulation of debt has taken for ever out of our power those easy sources of revenue, which, applied to the ordinary necessities and exigencies of Government, would have answered them habitually, and covered us from habitual murmerings against taxes & tax gatherers; reserving extraordinary calls, for extraordinary occasions, would animate the People to meet them.

3d.   That the calls for money have been no greater than we must generally expect, for the same or equivalent exigencies; yet we are already obliged to strain the *impost* till it produces clamour, and will produce evasion, and war on our citizens to collect it, and even to resort to an *Excise* law, of odious character with the people; partial in its operation; unproductive unless enforced by arbitrary & vexatious means; and committing the authority of the Government in parts where resistance is most probable, & coercion least practicable.

4th.   They cite propositions in Congress, and suspect other projects on foot, still to encrease the mass of the debt.

Harold C. Syrett et al., eds., *The Papers of Alexander Hamilton,* 27 vols. (New York: Columbia University Press, 1961–87), 12:129–33.

5th.   They say that by borrowing at 2/3 of the interest, we might have paid of[f] the principal in 2/3 of the time; but that from this we are precluded by its being made irredeemable but in small portions, & long terms.

6th.   That this irredeemable quality was given it for the avowed purpose of inviting its transfer to foreign Countries.

7th.   They predict that this transfer of the principal, when compleated, will occasion an exportation of 3 Millions of dollars annually for the interest; a drain of Coin, of which as there has been no example, no calculation can be made of its consequences.

8th.   That the banishment of our Coin will be compleated by the creation of 10 millions of paper money, in the form of Bank-bills now issuing into circulation.

9th.   They think the 10 or 12 pr Ct. annual profit, paid to the lenders of this paper medium, are taken out of the pockets of the people, who would have had without interest the coin it is banishing.

10th.   That all the Capitol employed in paper speculation is barren & useless, producing, like that on a gaming table, no accession to itself, and is withdrawn from Commerce and Agriculture where it would have produced addition to the common mass.

11th.   That it nourishes in our citizens vice & idleness instead of industry & morality.

12th.   That it has furnished effectual means of corrupting such a portion of the legislature, as turns the balance between the honest Voters which ever way it is directed.

13th.   That this corrupt squadron, deciding the voice of the legislature, have manifested their dispositions to get rid of the limitations imposed by the Constitution on the general legislature; limitations, on the faith of which, the States acceded to that instrument.

14th.   That the ultimate object of all this is to prepare the way for a change, from the present republican form of Government, to that of a monarchy; of which the British Constitution is to be the model.

15th.   That this was contemplated in the Convention, they say is no secret, because its partisans have made none of it — to effect it then was impracticable; but they are still eager after their object, and are predisposing every thing for its ultimate attainment.

16th.   So many of them have got into the legislature, that, aided by the corrupt squadron of paper dealers, who are at their devotion, they make a majority in both houses.

17th.   The republican party who wish to preserve the Government in its present form, are fewer even when joined by the two, three, or half a dozen antifederalists, who, tho' they dare not avow it, are still opposed to any general Government: but being less so to a republican than a Monarchical one, they naturally join those whom they think pursuing the lesser evil.

18th.   Of all the mischiefs objected to the system of measures before-mentioned, none they add is so afflicting, & fatal to every honest hope, as the corruption of the legislature. As it was the earliest of these measures it became the instrument for producing the rest, and will be the instrument for producing in future a King, Lords & Commons; or whatever else those who direct it may chuse. Withdrawn such a distance from the eye of their Constituents, and these so dispersed as to be inaccessible to public information, and particularly to that of the conduct of their own Representatives, they will form the worst Government upon earth, if the means of their corruption be not prevented.

19th.   The only hope of safety they say, hangs now on the numerous representation which is to come forward the ensuing year; but should the majority of the new members be still in the same principles with the present — shew so much deriliction to republican government, and such a disposition to encroach upon, or explain away the limited powers of the constitution in order to change it, it is not easy to conjecture what would be the result, nor what means would be resorted to for correction of the evil. True wisdom they acknowledge should direct temperate & peaceable measures; but add, the division of sentiment & interest happens unfortunately, to be so geographical, that no mortal can say that what is most wise & temperate, would prevail against what is more easy & obvious; they declare, they can contemplate no evil more incalculable than the breaking of the Union into two, or more parts; yet, when they view the mass which opposed the original coalescence, when they consider that it lay chiefly in the Southern quarter — that the legislature have availed themselves of no occasion of allaying it, but on the contrary whenever Northern & Southern prejudices have come into conflict, the latter have been sacraficed and the former soothed.

20th.   That the owers of the debt are in the Southern and the holders of it in the Northern division.

21st.   That the antifederal champions are now strengthened in argument by the fulfilment of their predictions, which has been brought about by the Monarchical federalists themselves; who, having been for the new government merely as a stepping stone to Monarchy, have themselves adopted the very construction, of which, when advocating its acceptance before the tribunal of the people, they declared it insuceptable; whilst the republican federalists, who espoused the same government for its intrinsic merits, are disarmed of their weapons, that which they denied as prophecy being now become true history. Who, therefore, can be sure they ask, that these things may not proselyte the small number which was wanting to place the majority on the other side — and this they add is the event at which they tremble.

These, as well as my memory serves me, are the sentiments which, directly and indirectly, have been disclosed to me.

To obtain light, and to pursue truth, being my sole aim; and wishing to have before me *explanations* of as well as the *complaints* on measures in which the public interest, harmony and peace is so deeply concerned, and my public conduct so much involved; it is my request, and you would oblige me in furnishing me, with your ideas upon the discontents here enumerated — and for this purpose I have thrown them into heads or sections, and numbered them that those ideas may apply to the corrispondent numbers. Although I do not mean to hurry you in giving your thoughts on the occasion of this letter, yet, as soon as you can make it convenient to yourself it would — for more reasons than one — be agreeable, & very satisfactory to me. . . .

At about the same time that Jefferson revealed his frustrations to Washington, Hamilton was writing to Edward Carrington, a Virginia Federalist, "to unbosom myself . . . on the present state of political parties and views," as he explained to this friend from Revolutionary War days. As a lieutenant colonel, Carrington had served with Hamilton on Washington's staff. Working together on missions for General Washington, they became lifelong friends. Hamilton's letter to Carrington was not only of extraordinary length but also one of the most revealing commentaries that Hamilton ever penned. In it he displayed not only his opposition to Jefferson, but also his resentment of Madison's growing disaffection with the policies of Washington's administration, in general, and of Hamilton, in particular.

ALEXANDER HAMILTON

Letter to Edward Carrington

May 26, 1792

PHILADELPHIA MAY 26TH, 1792.

My dear Sir:

Believing that I possess a share of your personal friendship and confidence and yielding to that which I feel towards you — persuaded also

Harold C. Syrett et al., eds., *The Papers of Alexander Hamilton,* 27 vols. (New York: Columbia University Press, 1961–87), 11:426–45.

that our political creed is the same on *two essential points,* 1st the necessity of *Union* to the respectability and happiness of this Country and 2 the necessity of an *efficient* general government to maintain that Union — I have concluded to unbosom myself to you on the present state of political parties and views. I ask no reply to what I shall say. I only ask that you will be persuaded, the representations I shall make are agreable to the real and sincere impressions of my mind. You will make the due allowances for the influence of circumstances upon it — you will consult your own observations and you will draw such a conclusion as shall appear to you proper. . . .

It was not 'till the last session that I became unequivocally convinced of the following truth — *"That Mr. Madison cooperating with Mr. Jefferson is at the head of a faction decidedly hostile to me and my administration, and actuated by views in my judgment subversive of the principles of good government and dangerous to the union, peace and happiness of the Country."*

These are strong expressions; they may pain your friendship for one or both of the Gentlemen whom I have named. I have not lightly resolved to hazard them. They are the result of a *Serious alarm* in my mind for the public welfare, and of a full conviction that what I have alledged is a truth, and a truth, which ought to be told and well attended to, by all the friends of Union and efficient National Government. The suggestion will, I hope, at least awaken attention, free from the byass of former prepossessions.

This conviction in my mind is the result of a long train of circumstances; many of them minute. To attempt to detail them all would fill a volume. I shall therefore confine myself to the mention of a few.

First — As to the point of opposition to me and my administration.

Mr. Jefferson with very little reserve manifests his dislike of the funding system generally; calling in question the expediency of funding a debt at all. Some expressions which he has dropped in my own presence (sometimes without sufficient attention to delicacy) will not permit me to doubt on this point, representations, which I have had from various respectable quarters. I do not mean, that he advocates directly the undoing of what has been done, but he censures the whole on principles, which if they should become general, could not but end in the subversion of the system.

In various conversations with *foreigners* as well as citizens, he has thrown censure on my *principles* of government and on my measures of administration. He has predicted that the people would not long tolerate my proceedings & that I should not long maintain my ground. Some of those, whom he *immediately* and *notoriously* moves, have *even* whispered suspicions of the rectitude of my motives and conduct. In the question concerning the Bank he not only delivered an opinion in writing against its constitutionality & expediency; but he did it *in a stile and manner* which I felt as partaking of asperity and ill humour towards me. As one of the trustees of the sinking fund,[5] I have experienced in almost every

---

[5] A fund accumulated to pay off a debt when it is due.

leading question opposition from him. When any turn of things in the community has threatened either odium or embarrassment to me, he has not been able to suppress the satisfaction which it gave him.

A part of this is of course information, and might be misrepresentation. But it comes through so many channels and so well accords with what falls under my own observation that I can entertain no doubt.

I find a strong confirmation in the following circumstances. *Freneau* the present Printer of the National Gazette, who was a journeyman with Childs & Swain at New York, was a known anti-federalist. It is reduced to a certainty that he was brought to Philadelphia by Mr. Jefferson to be the conductor of a News Paper. It is notorious that cotemporarily with the commencement of his paper he was a Clerk in the department of state for foreign languages. Hence a clear inference that his paper has been set on foot and is conducted under the patronage & not against the views of Mr. Jefferson. What then is the complexion of this paper? Let any impartial man peruse all the numbers down to the present day; and I never was more mistaken, if he does not pronounce that it is a paper devoted to the subversion of me & the measures in which I have had an Agency; and I am little less mistaken if he do not pronounce that it is a paper of a tendency *generally unfriendly* to the Government of the U States.

It may be said, that a News Paper being open to all the publications, which are offered to it, its complexion may be influenced by other views than those of the Editor. But the fact here is that wherever the Editor appears it is in a correspondent dress. The paragraphs which appear as his own, the publications, not original which are selected for his press, are of the same malignant and unfriendly aspect, so as not to leave a doubt of the temper which directs the publication.

Again [Andrew] *Brown,* who publishes an Evening paper called *The Federal Gazette* was originally a zealous federalist and personally friendly to me. He has been employed by Mr. Jefferson as a Printer to the Government for the publication of the laws; and for some time past 'till lately the complexion of his press was equally bitter and unfriendly to me & to the Government. . . . Thus far, as to Mr. Jefferson.

With regard to Mr. Madison — the matter stands thus. I have not heard, but in the one instance to which I have alluded, of his having held language unfriendly to me in private conversation. But in his public conduct there has been a more uniform & persevering opposition than I have been able to resolve into a sincere difference of opinion. I cannot persuade myself that Mr. Madison and I, whose politics had formerly so much the *same point of departure,* should now diverge so widely in our opinions of the measures which are proper to be pursued. The opinion I once entertained of the candour and simplicity and fairness of Mr. Madisons character has, I acknowledge, given way to a decided opinion that *it is one of a peculiarly artificial and complicated kind.* . . .

An intervening proof of Mr. Madisons unfriendly intrigues to my disadvantage is to be found in the following incident which I relate to you upon my honor but from the nature of it, you will perceive in the *strictest confidence.* The president having prepared his speech at the commencement of the ensuing session communicated it to Mr. Madison for his remarks. It contained among other things a *clause* concerning weights & measures, hinting the advantage of an invariable standard, which *preceded,* in the original state of the speech, a clause concerning the Mint. Mr. Madison suggested a transposition of these clauses & the addition of certain words, which I now forget importing an *immediate connection* between the two subjects. You may recollect that Mr. Jefferson proposes that the *unit of weight* & the *unit in the coins* shall be the same, & that my propositions are to preserve the Dollar as the Unit, adhering to its present quantity of Silver, & establishing the same proportion of alloy in the silver as in the gold Coins. The evident design of this manoeuvre was to connect the Presidents opinion in favour of Mr. Jefferson's idea, in contradiction to mine, &, the worst of it is, *without his being aware of the tendency of the thing.* It happened, that the President shewed me the Speech, altered in conformity to Mr. Madisons suggestion, just before it was copied for the purpose of being delivered. I remarked to him the tendency of the alteration. *He declared that he had not been aware of it & had no such intention; & without hesitation agreed to expunge the words which were designed to connect the two subjects.*

This transaction, in my opinion, not only furnishes a proof of Mr. Madisons *intrigues,* in opposition to my measures, but charges him with an *abuse* of the Presidents confidence in him, by endeavouring to make him, without his knowledge, take part with one officer against another, in a case in which they had given different opinions to the Legislature of the Country. *I forbore to awaken the President's mind to this last inference;* but it is among the circumstances which have convinced me that Mr. Madisons true character is the reverse of that *simple, fair, candid one,* which he has assumed.

I have informed you, that Mr. Freneau was brought to Philadelphia, by Mr. Jefferson, to be the Conductor of a News Paper. My information announced Mr. Madison as the mean of negotiation while he was at New York last summer. This and the general coincidence & close intimacy between the two Gentlemen leave no doubt that their views are substantially the same. . . .

In almost all the questions great & small which have arisen, since the first session of Congress, Mr. Jefferson & Mr. Madison have been found among those who were disposed to narrow the Federal authority. The question of a National Bank is one example. The question of bounties to the Fisheries is another. Mr. Madison resisted it on the ground of constitutionality, 'till it was evident, by the intermediate questions taken, that the bill would pass & he then under the wretched subterfuge of a change of a single word "bounty" for "allowance" went over to the Majority & voted for the bill. In the Militia bill & in a variety of minor cases he has leaned to abridging the exercise of fœderal authority, & leaving as much as possible to the States & he has lost no opportunity of *sounding the alarm* with great affected solemnity at encroachments meditated on the rights of the States, & of holding up the bugbear of a faction in the Government having designs unfriendly to Liberty.

This kind of conduct has appeared to me the more extraordinary on the part of Mr. Madison as I know for a certainty it was a primary article in his Creed that the real danger in our system was the subversion of the National authority by the preponderancy of the State Governments. All his measures have proceeded on an opposite supposition.

I recur again to the instance of Freneaus paper. In matters of this kind one cannot have direct proof of men's latent views; they must be inferred from circumstances. As the coadjutor of Mr. Jefferson in the establishment of this paper, I include Mr. Madison in the consequences imputable to it.

In respect to our foreign politics the views of these Gentlemen are in my judgment equally unsound & dangerous. *They have a womanish attachment to France and a womanish resentment against Great Britain.* They would draw us into the closest embrace of the former & involve us in all the consequences of her politics, & they would risk the peace of the country in their endeavours to keep us at the greatest possible distance from the latter. This disposition goes to a length particularly in Mr. Jefferson of which, till lately, I had no adequate Idea. Various circumstances prove to me that if these Gentlemen were left to pursue their own course there would be in less than six months *an open War between the U States & Great Britain.*

I trust I have a due sense of the conduct of France towards this Country in the late Revolution, & that I shall always be among the foremost in making her every suitable return; but there is a wide difference between this & implicating ourselves in all her politics; between bearing good will to her, & hating and wranggling with all those whom she hates. The Neutral & the Pacific Policy appear to me to mark the true path to the U States.

Having now delineated to you what I conceive to be the true complexion of the politics of these Gentlemen, I will now attempt a solution of these strange appearances.

Mr. Jefferson, it is known, did not in the first instance cordially acquiesce in the new constitution for the U States; he had many doubts & reserves. He left this Country before we had experienced the imbicillities of the former.

In France he saw government only on the side of its abuses. He drank deeply of the French Philosophy, in Religion, in Science, in politics. He came from France in the moment of a fermentation which he had had a share in exciting, & in the passions and feelings of which he shared both from temperament and situation.

He came here probably with a too partial idea of his own powers, and with the expectation of a greater share in the direction of our councils than he has in reality enjoyed. I am not sure that he had not peculiarly marked out for himself the department of the Finances.

He came electrified *plus* with attachment to France and with the project of knitting together the two Countries in the closest political bands.

Mr. Madison had always entertained an exalted opinion of the talents, knowledge and virtues of Mr. Jefferson. The sentiment was probably reciprocal. A close correspondence subsisted between them during the time of Mr. Jefferson's absence from this country. A close intimacy arose upon his return.

Whether any peculiar opinions of Mr. Jefferson concerning the public debt wrought a change in the sentiments of Mr. Madison (for it is certain that the former is more radically wrong than the latter) or whether Mr. Madison seduced by the expectation of popularity and possibly by the calculation of advantage to the state of Virginia was led to change his own opinion — certain it is, that a very material *change* took place, & that the two Gentlemen were united in the new ideas. Mr. Jefferson was indiscreetly open in his approbation of Mr. Madison's principles, upon his first coming to the seat of Government. I say indiscreetly, because a Gentleman in the administration in one department ought not to have taken sides against another, in another department.

The course of this business & a variety of circumstances which took place left Mr. Madison a very discontented & chagrined man and begot some degree of ill humour in Mr. Jefferson.

Attempts were made by these Gentlemen in different ways to produce a Commercial Warfare with Great Britain. In this too they were disappointed. And as they had the liveliest wishes on the subject their dissatisfaction has been proportionally great; and as I had not favoured the project, I was comprehended in their displeasure.

These causes and perhaps some others created, much sooner than I was aware of it, a systematic opposition to me on the part of those Gentlemen. My subversion, I am now satisfied, has been long an object with them.

Subsequent events have encreased the Spirit of opposition and the feelings of personal mortification on the part of these Gentlemen.

A mighty stand was made on the affair of the Bank. There was much *commitment* in that case. I prevailed. . . .

Another circumstance has contributed to widening the breach. 'Tis evident beyond a question, from every movement, that Mr. Jefferson aims with ardent desire at the Presidential Chair. This too is an important object of the party-politics. It is supposed, from the nature of my former personal & political connexions, that I may favour some other candidate more than Mr. Jefferson when the Question shall occur by the retreat of the present Gentleman. My influence therefore with the Community becomes a thing, on ambitious & personal grounds, to be resisted & destroyed.

You know how much it was a point to establish the Secretary of State as the Officer who was to administer the Government in defect of[6] the President & Vice President. Here I acknowledge, though I took far less part than was supposed, I run counter to Mr. Jefferson's wishes; but if I had had no other reason for it, I had already *experienced opposition* from him which rendered it a measure of *self defence.*

It is possible too (for men easily heat their imaginations when their passions are heated) that they have by degrees persuaded themselves of what they may have at first only sported to influence others — namely that there is some dreadful combination against State Government & republicanism; which according to them, are convertible terms. But there is so much absurdity in this supposition, that the admission of it tends to apologize for their hearts, at the expence of their heads.

Under the influence of all these circumstances, the attachment to the Government of the U States originally weak in Mr. Jeffersons mind has given way to something very like dislike; in Mr. Madisons, it is so counteracted by personal feelings, as to be more an affair of the head than of the heart — more the result of a conviction of the necessity of Union than of cordiality to the thing itself. I hope it does not stand worse than this with him. . . .

A word on another point. I am told that serious apprehensions are disseminated in your state as to the existence of a Monarchical party meditating the destruction of State & Republican Government. If it is possible that so absurd an idea can gain ground it is necessary that it should be combatted. I assure you on my *private faith* and *honor* as a Man that there is not in my judgment a shadow of foundation of it. A very small number of men indeed may entertain theories less republican than Mr Jefferson & Mr. Madison; but I am persuaded there is not a Man among them who would not regard as both *criminal & visionary*[7] any attempt to subvert the republican system of the Country. Most of these men rather *fear* that it may not justify itself by its fruits, than feel a predilection for a different form; and their fears are not diminished by the factions & fanatical politics which they find prevailing among a certain set of Gentlemen and threatening to disturb the tranquillity and order of the Government.

As to the destruction of State Governments, the *great* and *real* anxiety is to be able to preserve the National from the too potent and counteracting influence of those Governments. As to my own political Creed, I give it to you with the utmost sincerity. I am *affectionately* attached to the

---

[6] in defect of: in absence of.
[7] visionary: illusory.

Republican theory. I desire *above all things* to see the *equality* of political rights exclusive of all *hereditary* distinction firmly established by a practical demonstration of its being consistent with the order and happiness of society.

As to State Governments, the prevailing byass of my judgment is that if they can be circumscribed within bounds consistent with the preservation of the National Government they will prove useful and salutary. If the States were all of the size of Connecticut, Maryland or New Jersey, I should decidedly regard the local Governments as both safe & useful. As the thing now is, however, I acknowledge the most serious apprehensions that the Government of the U States will not be able to maintain itself against their influence. I see that influence already penetrating into the National Councils & preverting their direction.

Hence a disposition on my part towards a liberal construction of the powers of the National Government and to erect every fence to guard it from depredations, which is, in my opinion, consistent with constitutional propriety.

As to any combination to prostrate the State Governments I disavow and deny it. From an apprehension lest the Judiciary should not work efficiently or harmoniously I have been desirous of seeing some rational scheme of connection adopted as an amendment to the constitution, otherwise I am for maintaining things as they are, though I doubt much the possibility of it, from a tendency in the nature of things towards the preponderancy of the State Governments.

I said, that I was *affectionately* attached to the Republican theory. This is the real language of my heart which I open to you in the sincerity of friendship; & I add that I have strong hopes of the success of that theory; but in candor I ought also to add that I am far from being without doubts. I consider its success as yet a problem.

It is yet to be determined by experience whether it be consistent with that *stability* and *order* in Government which are essential to public strength & private security and happiness. On the whole, the only enemy which Republicanism has to fear in this Country is in the Spirit of faction and anarchy. If this will not permit the ends of Government to be attained under it — if it engenders disorders in the community, all regular & orderly minds will wish for a change — and the demagogues who have produced the disorder will make it for their own aggrandizement. This is the old Story.

If I were disposed to promote Monarchy & overthrow State Governments, I would mount the hobby horse of popularity — I would cry out usurpation — danger to liberty &c. &c — I would endeavour to prostrate the National Government — raise a ferment — and then "ride in the Whirlwind and direct the Storm." That there are men acting with Jefferson & Madison who have this in view I verily believe. I could lay my finger on some of them. That Madison does *not* mean it I also verily believe, and

I rather believe the same of Jefferson; but I read him upon the whole thus — "A man of profound ambition & violent passions."

You must be by this time tired of my epistle. Perhaps I have treated certain characters with too much severity. I have however not meant to do them injustice — and from the bottom of my soul believe I have drawn them truly and that it is of the utmost consequence to the public weal they should be viewed in their true colors. I yield to this impression. I will only add that I make no clandestine attacks on the gentlemen concerned. They are both apprized indirectly from myself of the opinion I entertain of their views. With the truest regard and esteem.

In response to Washington's letter of July 29, 1792, Hamilton composed a reply too lengthy to be included here. In that letter, he answered Washington point by point and refuted or denied most of the charges while defending his own policies.[8] When Washington thanked Hamilton for the detailed paper, he indicated that he had not been able to give it "the attentive reading I mean to bestow," but he expected to "receive both satisfaction and profit from the perusal." In this private letter, the president also called for more harmony within his cabinet. "Differences in political opinions are as unavoidable as, to a certain point, they may perhaps be necessary," he wrote, but he regretted that subjects could not be discussed without impugning the motives of opponents. He expressed his hope that "liberal allowances will be made for the political opinions of one another; and instead of wounding suspicions, and irritating charges . . . there might be mutual forbearances and temporising yieldings *on all sides.*"[9]

Washington wrote similarly to Jefferson, calling for "more charity for the opinions and acts of one another in Governmental matters." He pleaded, "My earnest wish, and my fondest hope therefore is, that instead of wounding suspicions, and irritable charges, there may be liberal allowances — mutual forbearances — and temporising yieldings on *all sides.*" He wrote that he had given the same advice to other officers of the government "because the disagreements which have arisen from differ-

---

[8] Hamilton to Washington, Aug. 18, 1792, in Harold C. Syrett et al., eds., *The Papers of Alexander Hamilton,* 27 vols. (New York: Columbia University Press (1961–87), 12: 228–58.

[9] Washington to Hamilton, Aug. 26, 1792, ibid., pp. 276–77.

ence of opinions, and the Attacks which have been made upon almost all the measures of government, and most of its Executive Officers, have, for a long time past, filled me with painful sensations; and cannot fail I think, of producing unhappy consequences at home and abroad."[10]

By coincidence, Hamilton, in Philadelphia, and Jefferson, at Monticello, replied to Washington on the same day — September 9, 1792 — Jefferson writing at far greater length than Hamilton.

[10]Washington to Jefferson, Aug. 23, 1792, in Boyd, Cullen, and Catanzariti, eds., *Jefferson Papers*, 24:317.

ALEXANDER HAMILTON

Letter to George Washington

September 9, 1792

PHILADELPHIA SEPTEMBER 9, 1792.

Sir:

I have the pleasure of your private letter of the 26th of August.

The feelings and views which are manifested in that letter are such as I expected would exist. And I most sincerely regret the causes of the uneasy sensations you experience. It is my most anxious wish, as far as may depend upon me, to smooth the path of your administration, and to render it prosperous and happy. And if any prospect shall open of healing or terminating the differences which exist, I shall most chearfully embrace it; though I consider myself as the deeply injured party. The recommendation of such a spirit is worthy of the moderation and wisdom which dictated it; and if your endeavours should prove unsucessful, I do not hesitate to say that in my opinion the period is not remote when the public good will require *substitutes* for the *differing members* of your administration. The continuance of a division there must destroy the energy of Government, which will be little enough with the strictest Union. On my part there will be a most chearful acquiescence in such a result.

I trust, Sir, that the greatest frankness has always marked and will always mark every step of my conduct towards you. In this disposition, I cannot conceal from you that I have had some instrumentality of late in the retaliations which have fallen upon certain public characters and that I find myself placed in a situation not to be able to recede *for the present.*

Harold C. Syrett et al., eds., *The Papers of Alexander Hamilton,* 27 vols. (New York: Columbia University Press, 1961–87), 12:347–50.

I considered myself as compelled to this conduct by reasons public as well as personal of the most cogent nature. I *know* that I have been an object of uniform opposition from Mr. Jefferson, from the first moment of his coming to the City of New York to enter upon his present office. I *know*, from the most authentic sources, that I have been the frequent subject of the most unkind whispers and insinuating from the same quarter. I have long seen a formed party in the Legislature, under his auspices, bent upon my subversion. I cannot doubt, from the evidence I possess, that the National Gazette was instituted by him for political purposes and that one leading object of it has been to render me and all the measures connected with my department as odious as possible.

Nevertheless I can truly say, that, except explanations to confidential friends, I never directly or indirectly retaliated or countenanced retaliation till very lately. I can even assure you, that I was instrumental in preventing a very severe and systematic attack upon Mr. Jefferson, by an association of two or three individuals, in consequence of the persecution, which he brought upon the Vice President, by his indiscreet and light letter to the Printer, transmitting *Paine's* pamphlet.

As long as I saw no danger to the Government, from the machinations which were going on, I resolved to be a silent sufferer of the injuries which were done me. I determined to avoid giving occasion to any thing which could manifest to the world dissentions among the principal characters of the government; a thing which can never happen without weakening its hands, and in some degree throwing a stigma upon it.

But when I no longer doubted, that there was a formed party deliberately bent upon the subversion of measures, which in its consequences would subvert the Government—when I saw, that the undoing of the funding system in particular (which, whatever may be the original merits of that system, would prostrate the credit and the honor of the Nation, and bring the Government into contempt with that description of Men, who are in every society the only firm supporters of government) was an avowed object of the party; and that all possible pains were taking to produce that effect by rendering it odious to the body of the people — I considered it as a duty, to endeavour to resist the torrent, and as an essential mean to this end, to draw aside the veil from the principal Actors. To this strong impulse, to this decided conviction, I have yielded. And I think events will prove that I have judged rightly.

Nevertheless I pledge my honor to you Sir, that if you shall hereafter form a plan to reunite the members of your administration, upon some steady principle of cooperation, I will faithfully concur in executing it during my continuance in office. And I will not directly or indirectly say or do a thing, that shall endanger a feud.

I have had it very much at heart to make an excursion to Mount Vernon, by way of the Fœderal City [future Washington, D.C.] in the course of this Month — and have been more than once on the point of asking your permission for it. But I now despair of being able to effect it. I am nevertheless equally obliged by your kind invitation.

The subject mentioned in the Postscript of your letter shall with great pleasure be carefully attended to. With the most faithful and affectionate attachment I have the honor to remain

Sir   Your most Obed & humble servant   A HAMILTON

THOMAS JEFFERSON

Letter to George Washington

September 9, 1792

MONTICELLO SEP. 9, 1792.

Dear Sir:

I received on the 2d. inst[10] the letter of Aug. 23. which you did me the honor to write me; but the immediate return of our post, contrary to his[11] custom, prevented my answer by that occasion. . . .

I now take the liberty of proceeding to that part of your letter wherein you notice the internal dissentions which have taken place within our government, and their disagreeable effect on it's movements. That such dissentions have taken place is certain, and even among those who are nearest to you in the administration. To no one have they given deeper concern than myself; to no one equal mortification at being myself a part of them. Tho' I take to myself no more than my share of the general observations of your letter, yet I am so desirous ever that you should know the whole truth, and believe no more than the truth, that I am glad to seize every occasion of developing to you whatever I do or think relative to the government; and shall therefore ask permission to be more lengthy now than the occasion particularly calls for, or would otherwise perhaps justify.

When I embarked in the government, it was with a determination to intermeddle not at all with the legislature, and as little as possible with my co-departments. The first and only instance of variance from the former part of my resolution, I was duped into by the Secretary of the treasury, and made a tool for forwarding his schemes, not then sufficiently understood by me; and of all the errors of my political life, this has occasioned

[10] inst: present or current month.
[11] his: the mail carrier.

Julian P. Boyd, Charles T. Cullen, and John Catanzariti, eds., *The Papers of Thomas Jefferson,* 27 vols. to date (Princeton: Princeton University Press, 1950–), 24:351–59.

me the deepest regret.[12] It has ever been my purpose to explain this to you, when, from being actors on the scene, we shall have become uninterested spectators only. The second part of my resolution has been religiously observed with the war department; and as to that of the Treasury, has never been farther swerved from, than by the mere enunciation of my sentiments in conversation, and chiefly among those who, expressing the same sentiments, drew mine from me. If it has been supposed that I have ever intrigued among the members of the legislature to defeat the plans of the Secretary of the Treasury, it is contrary to all truth. As I never had the desire to influence the members, so neither had I any other means than my friendships, which I valued too highly to risk by usurpations on their freedom of judgment, and the conscientious pursuit of their own sense of duty. That I have utterly, in my private conversations, disapproved of the system of the Secretary of the treasury, I acknolege and avow: and this was not merely a speculative difference. His system flowed from principles adverse to liberty, and was calculated to undermine and demolish the republic, by creating an influence of his department over the members of the legislature. I saw this influence actually produced, and it's first fruits to be the establishment of the great outlines of his project by the votes of the very persons who, having swallowed his bait were laying themselves out to profit by his plans: and that had these persons withdrawn, as those interested in a question ever should, the vote of the disinterested majority was clearly the reverse of what they made it. These were no longer the votes then of the representatives of the people, but of deserters from the rights and interests of the people: and it was impossible to consider their decisions, which had nothing in view but to enrich themselves, as the measures of the fair majority, which ought always to be respected.— If what was actually doing begat uneasiness in those who wished for virtuous government, what was further proposed was not less threatening to the friends of the constitution. For, in a Report on the subject of manufactures, (still to be acted on) it was expressly assumed that the general government has a right to exercise all powers which may be for the *general welfare,* that is to say, all the legitimate powers of government: since no government has a legitimate right to do what is not for the welfare of the governed. There was indeed a sham-limitation of the universality of this power *to cases where money is to be employed.* But about what is it that money cannot be employed? Thus the object of these plans taken together is to draw all the powers of government into the hands of the general legislature, to establish means for corrupting a sufficient corps in that legislature to divide the honest votes and preponderate, by their own, the scale which suited, and to have that corps under the command of the Secretary

---

[12]Jefferson refers to his role in the passage of the bill providing for the assumption of state debts by the national government and the locating of the national capital on the Potomac River.

of the Treasury for the purpose of subverting step by step the principles of the constitution, which he has so often declared to be a thing of nothing which must be changed. Such views might have justified something more than mere expressions of dissent, beyond which, nevertheless, I never went.—Has abstinence from the department committed to me been equally observed by him? To say nothing of other interferences equally known, in the case of the two nations with which we have the most intimate connections, France and England, my system was to give some satisfactory distinctions to the former, of little cost to us, in return for the solid advantages yeilded us by them; and to have met the English with some restrictions which might induce them to abate their severities against our commerce. I have always supposed this coincided with your sentiments. Yet the Secretary of the treasury, by his cabals with members of the legislature, and by high toned declamation on other occasions, has forced down his own system, which was exactly the reverse. He undertook, of his own authority, the conferences with the ministers of these two nations, and was, on every consultation, provided with some report of a conversation with the one or the other of them, adapted to his views. These views thus made to prevail, their execution fell of course to me; and I can safely appeal to you, who have seen all my letters and proceedings, whether I have not carried them into execution as sincerely as if they had been my own, tho' I ever considered them as inconsistent with the honor and interest of our country. That they have been inconsistent with our interest is but too fatally proved by the stab of our navigation given by the French.— So that if the question be By whose fault is it that Colo. Hamilton and myself have not drawn together? the answer will depend on that to two other questions; Whose principles of administration best justify, by their purity, conscientious adherence? and Which of us has, notwithstanding, stepped farthest into the controul of the department of the other?

To this justification of opinions, expressed in the way of conversation, against the views of Colo. Hamilton, I beg leave to add some notice of his late charges against me in Fenno's gazette: for neither the stile, matter, nor venom of the pieces alluded to can leave a doubt of their author. Spelling my name and character at full length to the public, while he conceals his own under the signature of "an American" he charges me 1. with having written letters from Europe to my friends to oppose the present constitution while depending.[13] 2. with a desire of not paying the public debt. 3. with setting up a paper to decry and slander the government. 1. The first charge is most false. No man in the U.S., I suppose, approved of every tittle in the constitution: no one, I believe approved more of it than I did: and more of it was certainly disapproved by my accuser than by me, and of it's

---

[13] depending: pending or under consideration.

parts most vitally republican. Of this the few letters I wrote on the subject (not half a dozen I believe) will be a proof: and for my own satisfaction and justification, I must tax you with the reading of them when I return to where they are. You will there see that my objection to the constitution was that it wanted a bill of rights securing freedom of religion, freedom of the press, freedom from standing armies, trial by jury, and a constant Habeas corpus act. Colo. Hamilton's was that it wanted a king and house of lords. The sense of America has approved by objection and added the bill of rights, not the king and lords. I also thought a longer term of service, insusceptible of renewal, would have made a President more independant. My country has thought otherwise, and I have acquiesced implicitly. He wished the general government should have power to make laws binding the states in all cases whatsoever. Our country has thought otherwise: has he acquiesced? Notwithstanding my wish for a bill of rights, my letters strongly urged the adoption of the constitution, by nine states at least, to secure the good it contained. I at first thought that the best method of securing the bill of rights would be for four states to hold off till such a bill should be agreed to. But the moment I saw Mr. Hancock's[14] proposition to pass the constitution as it stood, and give perpetual instructions to the representatives of every state to insist on a bill of rights, I acknoleged the superiority of his plan, and advocated universal adoption. 2. The second charge is equally untrue. My whole correspondence while in France, and every word, letter, and act on the subject since my return, prove that no man is more ardently intent to see the public debt soon and sacredly paid off than I am. This exactly marks the difference between Colo. Hamilton's views and mine, that I would wish the debt paid tomorrow; he wishes it never to be paid, but always to be a thing wherewith to corrupt and manage the legislature. 3. I have never enquired what number of sons, relations and friends of Senators, representatives, printers or other useful partisans Colo. Hamilton has provided for among the hundred clerks of his department, the thousand excisemen, customhouse officers, loan officers &c. &c. &c. appointed by him, or at his nod, and spread over the Union; nor could ever have imagined that the man who has the shuffling of millions backwards and forwards from paper into money and money into paper, from Europe to America, and America to Europe, the dealing out of Treasury-secrets among his friends in what time and measure he pleases, and who never slips an occasion of making friends with his means, that such an one I say would have brought forward a charge against me for having appointed the poet Freneau translating clerk to my office, with a salary of 250. dollars a year. . . .

Freneau's proposition to publish a paper, having been about the time that the writings of Publicola,[15] and the discourses on Davila had a good

[14]John Hancock made this proposal at the Massachusetts state ratifying convention.
[15]John Quincy Adams was the author of the writings of Publicola.

deal excited the public attention, I took for granted from Freneau's character, which had been marked as that of a good whig, that he would give free place to pieces written against the aristocratical and monarchical principles these papers had inculcated. This having been in my mind, it is likely enough I may have expressed it in conversation with others; tho' I do not recollect that I did. To Freneau I think I could not, because I had still seen him but once, and that was at a public table, at breakfast, at Mrs. Elsworth's, as I passed thro' New York the last year. And I can safely declare that my expectations looked only to the chastisement of the aristocratical and monarchical writers, and not to any criticisms on the proceedings of the government. Colo. Hamilton can see no motive for any appointment but that of making a convenient partisan. . . .

No government ought to be without censors: and where the press is free, no one ever will. If virtuous, it need not fear the fair operation of attack and defence. Nature has given to man no other means of sifting out the truth either in religion, law, or politics. I think it as honorable to the government neither to know, nor notice, it's sycophants or censors, as it would be undignified and criminal to pamper the former and persecute the latter. — So much for the past. A word now of the future.

When I came into this office, it was with a resolution to retire from it as soon as I could with decency. It pretty early appeared to me that the proper moment would be the first of those epochs at which the constitution seems to have contemplated a periodical change or renewal of the public servants. In this I was confirmed by your resolution respecting the same period; from which however I am happy in hoping you have departed. I look to that period with the longing of a wave-worn mariner, who has at length the land in view, and shall count the days and hours which still lie between me and it. In the mean while my main object will be to wind up the business of my office avoiding as much as possible all new enterprize. With the affairs of the legislature, as I never did intermeddle, so I certainly shall not now begin. I am more desirous to predispose every thing for the repose to which I am withdrawing, than expose it to be disturbed by newspaper contests. If these however cannot be avoided altogether, yet a regard for your quiet will be a sufficient motive for deferring it till I become merely a private citizen, when the propriety or impropriety of what I may say or do may fall on myself alone. I may then too avoid the charge of misapplying that time which now belonging to those who employ me, should be wholly devoted to their service. If my own justification, or the interests of the republic shall require it, I reserve to myself the right of then appealing to my country, subscribing my name to whatever I write, and using with freedom and truth the facts and names necessary to place the cause in it's just form before that tribunal. To a thorough disregard of the honors and emoluments of office, I join as great a value for the esteem of my countrymen; and conscious of having merited it by an integrity which cannot be reproached, and by an enthusiastic devotion to their rights and liberty, I will not suffer my retirement to be clouded by the slanders of a man whose history, from the moment at which history can stoop to notice him, is a tissue of machinations against the liberty of the country which has not only recieved and given him bread, but heaped it's honors on his head.— Still however I repeat the hope that it will not be necessary to make such an appeal. Though little known to the people of America, I believe that, as far as I am known, it is not as an enemy to the Republic, nor an intriguer against it, nor a waster of it's revenue, nor prostitutor of it to the purposes of corruption, as the American[16] represents me: and I confide that yourself are satisfied that, as to dissensions in the newspapers, not a syllable of them has ever proceeded from me; and that no cabals or intrigues of mine have produced those in the legislature; and I hope I may promise, both to you and myself, that none will recieve aliment from me during the short space I have to remain in office, which will find ample employment in closing the present business of the department. . . .

In the mean time and ever I am with great and sincere affection & respect, dear Sir, your most obedient and most humble servant

TH: JEFFERSON

The letters that passed between Jefferson and Washington and between Hamilton and Washington reveal the emergence of political parties in national politics. These divisions were clearer in Congress earlier than in most of the country. The development worried many political observers, who saw parties as divisive and a threat to the success of the new government.[17]

Despite their differences, one thing that Jefferson and Hamilton agreed on was that Washington should not retire from office, as he had planned, at the end of his four-year term as president. As Jefferson had written to Washington in May 1792, "The confidence of the whole union is centered in you. Your being at the helm, will be more than an answer to every argument which can be used to alarm and lead the people in any quarter into violence or secession. North and South will hang together, if they have you to hang on."[18] At the end of July 1792, Hamilton wrote the president that his "sounding of persons, whose opinions were worth

---

[16]The "American" was a series of essays by Hamilton published in the *Gazette of the United States* in August 1792.

[17]Noble E. Cunningham Jr., *The Jeffersonian Republicans: The Formation of Party Organization, 1789–1801* (Chapel Hill: University of North Carolina Press, 1957), pp. 20–21, 31–32, 75–76.

[18]Jefferson to Washington, May 23, 1792, in Boyd, Cullen, and Catanzariti, eds., *Jefferson Papers*, 23:535–40. Letter printed on pages 78–82 of this chapter.

knowing," convinced him that "the impression is uniform — that your declining would be deplored as the greatest evil, that could befall the country at the present juncture."[19]

Washington's consent to stand for reelection, followed by his election to a second term as president, influenced Jefferson to reconsider his plan to retire at the end of Washington's first term. That, however, was not the only consideration for continuing at his post. More important was Jefferson's concern that leaving office would be seen as retreating under attack from Hamilton and writers in the press.

Sometime early in 1793, Jefferson drafted the following resolutions designed to drive Hamilton from office as secretary of the Treasury. He expected the resolutions to be presented to the House of Representatives.

[19] Hamilton to Washington, July 30, 1792, in Syrett et al., eds., *Hamilton Papers,* 12:137.

THOMAS JEFFERSON

Resolutions on the Secretary of the Treasury

[Before February 27, 1793]

1. *Resolved,* That it is essential to the due administration of the Government of the United States, that laws making specific appropriations of money should be strictly observed by the Secretary of the Treasury thereof.

2. *Resolved,* That a violation of a law making appropriations of money is a violation of that section of the Constitution of the United States which requires that no money shall be drawn from the Treasury but in consequence of appropriations made by law.

3. *Resolved,* That the Secretary of the Treasury, in drawing to this country and lodging in the bank the funds raised in Europe, which ought to have been applied to the paiments of our debts there in order to stop interest, has violated the instructions of the President of the United States for the benefit of speculators and to increase the profits of that institution.

4. *Resolved,* That the Secretary of the Treasury has deviated from the instructions given by the President of the United States, in exceeding the authorities for making loans under the acts of the 4th and 12th of August, 1790.

Julian P. Boyd, Charles T. Cullen, and John Catanzariti, eds., *The Papers of Thomas Jefferson,* 27 vols. to date (Princeton: Princeton University Press, 1950–), 25:292–93.

5. *Resolved,* That the Secretary of the Treasury has omitted to discharge an essential duty of his office, in failing to give Congress official information in due time, of the moneys drawn by him from Europe into the United States; which drawing commenced December, 1790, and continued till January, 1793; and of the causes of making such drafts.

6. *Resolved,* That the Secretary of the Treasury has, without the instruction of the President of the United States, drawn more moneys borrowed in Holland into the United States than the President of the United States was authorized to draw, under the act of the 12th of August, 1790; which act appropriated two millions of dollars only, when borrowed, to the purchase of the Public Debt:[20] And that he has omitted to discharge an essential duty of his office, in failing to give official information to the Commissioners for purchasing the Public Debt, of the various sums drawn from time to time, suggested by him to have been intended for the purchase of the Public Debt.

7. *Resolved,* That the Secretary of the Treasury did not consult the public interest in negotiating a Loan with the Bank of the United States, and drawing therefrom four hundred thousand dollars, at five per cent. per annum, when a greater sum of public money was deposited in various banks at the respective periods of making the respective drafts.

8. *Resolved,* That the Secretary of the Treasury has been guilty of an indecorum to this House, in undertaking to judge of its motives in calling for information which was demandable of him, from the constitution of his office; and in failing to give all the necessary information within his knowledge, relatively to the subjects of the reference made to him of the 19th January, 1792, and of the 22d November, 1792, during the present session.

9. *Resolved,* That at the next meeting of Congress, the act of Sep 2d, 1789, establishing a Department of Treasury should be so amended as to constitute the office of the Treasurer of the United States a separate department, independent of the Secretary of the Treasury.

10. *Resolved,* That the Secretary of the Treasury has been guilty of maladministration in the duties of his office, and should, in the opinion of Congress, be removed from his office by the President of the United States.

Jefferson passed his proposed resolutions on to Representative William Branch Giles, a friendly Virginia Congressman. Giles, however, did not present the resolutions to the House of Representatives exactly as Jefferson had drafted them. Instead, on February 27, 1793, he proposed somewhat milder resolutions. Although including most of Jeffer-

[20] purchase of the Public Debt: redemption of the Public Debt.

son's charges, the resolutions, as revised by Giles, did not call for the removal of the secretary of the Treasury. Giles also omitted Jefferson's proposal that the Treasurer of the United States head a separate department independent of the secretary of the Treasury.[21]

All of Giles's resolutions were decisively voted down by the House of Representatives, and Hamilton continued in his post as secretary of the Treasury. Jefferson also stayed on through what would become his most trying year as secretary of state, and the conflict between Washington's two principal advisers continued.

[21] Boyd, Cullen, and Catanzariti, eds., *Jefferson Papers,* 25:294–96.

5

Disagreement on Foreign Affairs

Issues of financial and economic policies dominated much of President George Washington's first administration, but matters of foreign relations occupied the center of the nation's attention when Washington's second term began in 1793. As minister to France in 1789, Thomas Jefferson had watched in Paris "such events as will be for ever memorable in history," as he wrote to James Madison, expressing his high interest and support of the opening events of the French Revolution.[1] In America, Alexander Hamilton's reactions had indicated mixed feelings of support and concern, as indicated in the following letter to General Lafayette. (In 1781 Lt. Col. Hamilton had fought under General Lafayette in the Battle of Yorktown. In October 1789, Lafayette was in command of the French Revolutionary National Guard during the early months of the French Revolution.)

[1] Jefferson to Madison, July 22, 1789, in Julian P. Boyd, Charles T. Cullen, and John Catanzariti, eds., *The Papers of Thomas Jefferson,* 27 vols. to date (Princeton: Princeton University Press, 1950–), 15:299.

ALEXANDER HAMILTON

Letter to the Marquis de Lafayette

October 6, 1789

My Dear Marquis: NEW YORK OCTOBER 6TH. 1789.
I have seen with a mixture of Pleasure and apprehension the Progress of the events which have lately taken Place in your Country. As a friend to

Harold C. Syrett et al., eds., *The Papers of Alexander Hamilton,* 27 vols. (New York: Columbia University Press, 1961–87), 5:425.

mankind and to liberty I rejoice in the efforts which you are making to establish it while I fear much for the final success of the attempts, for the fate of those I esteem who are engaged in it, and for the danger in case of success of innovations greater than will consist with the real felicity of your Nation. If your affairs still go well, when this reaches you, you will ask why this foreboding of ill, when all the appearences have been so much in your favor. I will tell you; I dread disagreements among those who are now united (which will be likely to be improved by the adverse party) about the nature of your constitution; I dread the vehement character of your people, whom I fear you may find it more easy to bring on, than to keep within Proper bounds, after you have put them in motion; I dread the interested refractoriness of your nobles, who cannot all be gratified and who may be unwilling to submit to the requisite sacrifices. And I dread the reveries of your Philosophic politicians who appear in the moment to have great influence and who being mere speculatists may aim at more refinement than suits either with human nature or the composition of your Nation.

These my dear Marquis are my apprehensions. My wishes for your personal success and that of the cause of liberty are incessant. . . .

As secretary of state, Jefferson monitored closely the changes in France and the conflicts that they ignited in Europe. In a letter to his Virginia friend George Mason early in 1791, Jefferson assessed the progress of the revolution in France and its impact on other European countries and on the United States.

THOMAS JEFFERSON

Letter to George Mason

February 4, 1791

PHILADELPHIA FEB. 4. 1791.

Dear Sir:

I am to make you my acknowledgments for your favor of Jan. 10. and the information had from France which it contained. It confirmed what I had

---

Julian P. Boyd, Charles T. Cullen, and John Catanzariti, eds., *The Papers of Thomas Jefferson,* 27 vols. to date (Princeton: Princeton University Press, 1950–), 19:241.

heard more loosely before, and accounts still more recent are to the same effect. I look with great anxiety for the firm establishment of the new government in France, being perfectly convinced that if it takes place there, it will spread sooner or later all over Europe. On the contrary a check there would retard the revival of liberty in other countries. I consider the establishment and success of their government as necessary to stay up our own and to prevent it from falling back to that kind of Halfway-house, the English constitution. It cannot be denied that we have among us a sect who believe that to contain whatever is perfect in human institutions; that the members of this sect have, many of them, names and offices which stand high in the estimation of our countrymen. I still rely that the great mass of our community is untainted with these heresies, as is it's head. On this I build my hope that we have not laboured in vain, and that our experiment will still prove that men can be governed by reason. . . .

The alliance of Austria and Prussia against France led to a war, which before it ended brought the overthrow of Louis XVI, followed immediately by the proclamation of the French republic on September 21, 1792. When the news of these momentous events reached America in December, there was a tremendous outpouring of enthusiasm for the new republic. Many Americans saw the French people as following in the footsteps of the colonists who had revolted against George III in 1776.

Jefferson shared in this enthusiasm. He deplored the bloodshed in France but believed that the result was worth the cost. Early in 1793, in a letter to his friend William Short, U.S. minister to the Netherlands, Jefferson questioned Short's criticism of the violence in France.

THOMAS JEFFERSON

Letter to William Short

January 3, 1793

PHILADELPHIA JAN. 3. 1793.

Dear Sir:

My last private letter to you was of Oct. 16. . . . yesterday your private one of Sep. 15. came to hand. The tone of your letters had for some time given me pain, on account of the extreme warmth with which they censured the proceedings of the Jacobins of France. I considered that sect as the same with the Republican patriots. . . . In the struggle which was necessary, many guilty persons fell without the forms of trial, and with them some innocent. These I deplore as much as any body, and shall deplore some of them to the day of my death. But I deplore them as I should have done had they fallen in battle. It was necessary to use the arm of the people, a machine not quite so blind as balls and bombs, but blind to a certain degree. A few of their cordial friends met at their hands the fate of enemies. But time and truth will rescue and embalm their memories, while their posterity will be enjoying that very liberty for which they would never have hesitated to offer up their lives. The liberty of the whole earth was depending on the issue of the contest, and was ever such a prize won with so little innocent blood? My own affections have been deeply wounded by some of the martyrs to this cause, but rather than it should have failed, I would have seen half the earth desolated. Were there but an Adam and an Eve left in every country, and left free, it would be better than as it now is. I have expressed to you my sentiments, because they are really those of 99 in an hundred of our citizens. The universal feasts, and rejoicings which have lately been had on account of the successes of the French shewed the genuine effusions of their hearts. You have been wounded by the sufferings of your friends, and have by this circumstance been hurried into a temper of mind which would be extremely disrelished if known to your countrymen. The reserve of *the Prest. of the U.S.* had never permitted me to discover the light in which he viewed it, and as I was more anxious that you should satisfy him than me, I had still avoided explanations with you on the subject. . . .

Julian P. Boyd, Charles T. Cullen, and John Catanzariti, eds., *The Papers of Thomas Jefferson,* 27 vols. to date (Princeton: Princeton University Press, 1950–), 25:14.

Hamilton did not share Jefferson's justification for the violence in France. One scholarly biographer concluded that Hamilton "never wrote or spoke of the Revolution in France without registering the 'horror,' 'abhorrence' and 'repulsion' it excited in him."[2]

Toward the end of March 1793 — the month in which George Washington took the oath of office as president for a second term — news reached the United States that Louis XVI had been put on trial in France, condemned to death, and executed on January 21, 1793. Reports soon followed of the French declaration of war against Great Britain and Holland, and a month later news arrived of France's declaration of war against Spain.

The outbreak of fighting between France and Great Britain posed a critical problem for the United States. Was the alliance between France and the United States, made during the American Revolution, still in effect? President Washington cut short his spring vacation at Mount Vernon to return to Philadelphia to consult with his cabinet. Having sent ahead a list of questions for his advisers to consider, Washington assembled them on the morning after his arrival. The most important matters were whether a proclamation of neutrality should be issued and whether a minister from the French republic should be received. When Jefferson read the president's questions, he was convinced that although the handwriting was Washington's, the language and the doubts expressed were Hamilton's.[3]

Both Jefferson and Hamilton favored a policy of neutrality, but they differed strongly on who was to proclaim it. At a cabinet meeting on April 19, 1793, Jefferson argued that the president lacked the authority to issue a neutrality decree and that, in any event, it would be wiser to hold back and use any such declaration as a bargaining tool with Great Britain. Jefferson reasoned that Congress, having been granted power to declare war by the Constitution, had the power *not* to declare war. Therefore, Congress, not the president, should issue any declaration of neutrality. Hamilton, on the other hand, argued that the president's authority to conduct foreign affairs gave the president such power.

---

[2] John C. Miller, *Alexander Hamilton and the Growth of the New Nation* (New York: Harper and Row, 1964), p. 364.

[3] Noble E. Cunningham Jr., *In Pursuit of Reason: The Life of Thomas Jefferson* (Baton Rouge: Louisiana State University Press, 1987), pp. 180–81.

Jefferson's position was a minority one within the cabinet, but out of deference to his opinion the members agreed that the term *neutrality* should not be used, and Jefferson joined in the unanimous recommendation that the president issue such a proclamation. Washington clearly sided with Hamilton rather than Jefferson in this precedent-setting demonstration of the president's power to conduct foreign affairs, and on April 22, 1793, he issued a presidential declaration of neutrality — in which the word *neutrality* was not employed — drafted by Attorney General Edmund Randolph.[4]

At the cabinet meeting, Hamilton also proposed that the treaty with France be suspended, reasoning that the alliance had been made with the French monarchy, which no longer existed. The suspension of the treaty should last until it was clear what form the government of France would take. In opposing Hamilton's proposal, Jefferson insisted that treaties were made between nations, which had a right to change their governments, as the United States had done since the treaty of 1778 with France. The outcome of the cabinet deliberation was that the treaty was not suspended, but no steps were taken, nor proposed, to aid France. At the same time, it was evident that as a friendly neutral the United States would be of more help to France than as an ineffective military ally.

Meanwhile, Edmond Charles Genet, the newly appointed French minister to the United States, had landed in Charleston, South Carolina, and was on his way to Philadelphia. As minister to the United States, Genet's actions — en route and after arriving in the capital city — defied American neutrality. He boldly fitted out privateers and recruited Americans for military service. French privateers were soon bringing English prizes into American ports. By August 1793, both Jefferson and Hamilton were in agreement when the cabinet unanimously decided to demand Genet's recall.[5]

By that time, a problem more serious than Genet's undiplomatic conduct pervaded the city of Philadelphia: the plague of yellow fever. Before the disease abated in late November, the yellow fever took five thousand

[4] Cabinet meeting, Apr. 19, 1793, in Harold C. Syrett et al., eds., *The Papers of Alexander Hamilton,* 27 vols. (New York: Columbia University Press, 1961–87), 14:328, 308n; Jefferson to Madison, June 23, 30, 1793, in Boyd, Cullen, and Catanzariti, eds., *Jefferson Papers,* 26:346, 403.

[5] Cabinet meeting, Apr. 19, 1793, in Syrett et al., eds., *Hamilton Papers,* 14:328; Boyd, Cullen, and Catanzariti, eds., *Jefferson Papers,* 25:570–71.

lives. Both Alexander Hamilton and his wife contracted the fever but survived and went to New York to recover. Hamilton did not return to Philadelphia until the end of October.[6] Jefferson, who earlier had moved to a house outside the city, escaped the disease but left for Monticello in mid-September. He returned to Germantown — where Congress convened — on November 1 but did not go to Philadelphia until the end of November.

Jefferson had planned to resign as secretary of state at the end of Washington's first term as president in March 1793, but he stayed on until the end of December. Before leaving office, he completed a major report on commerce that he had been working on since 1791.[7] During his last month in office, Jefferson appears to have had little contact with Hamilton.

Returning to Monticello, Jefferson soon was feeling isolated from public affairs. After a month at home, he complained about the dearth of news and said that he had not seen a Philadelphia newspaper since he left the city. In mid-February 1794, he wrote to Madison that he "could not have supposed, when at Philadelphia, that so little of what was passing there could be known even in Kentucky, as is the case here."[8] By spring, Jefferson's interest in agriculture revived his spirits, and he began to profess more interest in farming than in politics. To John Adams, he wrote, "I return to farming with an ardour which I scarcely knew in my youth. . . . Instead of writing 10 or 12 letters a day, which I have been in the habit of doing as a thing of course, I put off answering my letters now, farmerlike, till a rainy day."[9]

Despite his disclaimers, Jefferson had not lost interest in public affairs. Although Alexander Hamilton was out of sight, he was not out of mind. Jefferson saw Hamilton's hand in the actions taken to suppress the Whiskey Rebellion in western Pennsylvania, when farmers' protests against the excise tax on whiskey led to open defiance of the law. In September 1794, Hamilton himself accompanied the troops into western

---

[6] Broadus Mitchell, *Alexander Hamilton: The National Adventure, 1788–1804* (New York: Macmillan, 1962), pp. 281–85.

[7] Boyd, Cullen, and Catanzariti, eds., *Jefferson Papers,* 27:532–80.

[8] Jefferson to Madison, Feb. 15, 1794, in James Morton Smith, ed., *The Republic of Letters: The Correspondence between Thomas Jefferson and James Madison, 1776–1826,* 3 vols. (New York: W. W. Norton, 1995), 2:831.

[9] Jefferson to Adams, Apr. 25, 1794, in Lester J. Cappon, ed., *The Adams-Jefferson Letters,* 2 vols. (Chapel Hill: University of North Carolina Press, 1959), 1:254.

Pennsylvania to quell the disorder. Jefferson later wrote disparagingly to James Monroe that "an insurrection was announced and proclaimed and armed against, but could never be found." [10]

By the end of 1794, the post of secretary of the Treasury no longer held the attraction for Hamilton that had existed earlier when many important decisions were being made and major national policies established. Routine matters of paying off the national debt and balancing the budget could be left to others. [11]

On January 16, 1795, Hamilton sent his final *Report on the Public Credit* to Congress, and on January 31, he resigned as the secretary of the Treasury. Out of office, Hamilton remained active in politics. In a letter to Madison in September 1795, Jefferson, who never fully understood all of Hamilton's financial manipulations, referred to Hamilton as "a colossus to the antirepublican party." [12] A year later, Madison wrote to Jefferson from Philadelphia,

> A committee of ways and means are employed in investigating our revenues and our wants. It is found that there are between six and seven millions of anticipations due to the Banks, that our ordinary income is barely at par with our ordinary expenditures, and that new taxes must be ready to meet near 1½ millions which will accrue in 1801. . . . Who could have supposed that Hamilton could have gone off in the triumph he assumed, with such a condition of the finances behind him? [13]

In reply to Madison, Jefferson wrote,

> I do not at all wonder at the condition in which the finances of the US are found. Ham's object from the beginning was to throw them into forms which should be utterly undecypherable. I ever said he did not understand their condition himself, nor was able to give a clear view of the excess of our debts beyond our credits, nor whether we were diminishing or increasing the debt. [14]

A major influence in Washington's administration as long as he remained in office, Hamilton continued to advise the president after resigning as secretary of the Treasury. When Washington decided to retire

---

[10] Jefferson to Monroe, May 26, 1795, in Paul L. Ford, ed., *The Works of Thomas Jefferson,* Federal Edition, 12 vols. (New York: G. P. Putnam's Sons, 1904), 8:177.

[11] Miller, *Hamilton,* pp. 436–37.

[12] Jefferson to Madison, Sept. 21, 1795, in Smith, ed., *Republic of Letters,* 2:897.

[13] Madison to Jefferson, Jan. 31, 1796, ibid., pp. 916–17.

[14] Jefferson to Madison, Mar. 6, 1796, ibid., p. 922.

from office at the end of his second term, it was Hamilton to whom he turned for help in drafting his farewell address.

As the contest to succeed Washington as president approached, Jefferson was reluctant to become a candidate. His Republican supporters, nevertheless, put him forward to oppose Vice President John Adams, who had the backing of the Federalists in the growing coalescence of early political parties. In the close election of 1796, the final electoral vote was 71 for Adams and 68 for Jefferson. Under the constitutional provisions then in force, Jefferson became vice president. He also became the expected challenger to Adams's anticipated bid for reelection in 1800. Meanwhile, in New York, Hamilton remained active in state politics and would soon again become a major figure on the national scene.

In returning to Philadelphia for the first time since he left the city in January 1794, Jefferson arrived at the seat of national government on March 2, 1797. On the following day, he was installed as the president of the American Philosophical Society, the first scientific society in America and the nation's leading intellectual organization, founded by Benjamin Franklin in 1743. On March 4, 1797, Jefferson was inaugurated as vice president of the United States. He remained in Philadelphia less than two weeks before leaving for Monticello, but he returned to Philadelphia on May 11 for a special session of Congress, called by President Adams in response to France's refusal to receive Charles Cotesworth Pinckney as the U.S. minister to France. In seeking to resolve this crisis, Adams appointed John Marshall and Elbridge Gerry to join Pinckney in negotiating with France. It was October before the commissioners arrived in Paris, and not until March 1798 did the president receive their report. That dispatch explained that they had been visited by agents (designated by President Adams in his later report to Congress as X, Y, and Z) of the French foreign minister, Talleyrand, who suggested that to open negotiation, a loan to France and a bribe of $240,000 was expected. The dispatch also reported the firm refusal of the American commissioners to accept such conditions.[15]

Congress responded to President Adams's report on these developments with increased military preparations. As military expansion accelerated, General Washington was called out of retirement to accept command of the army, though he agreed to take the field only in the event of

[15]Cunningham, *In Pursuit of Reason,* pp. 212–14.

an invasion by enemy forces. Upon Washington's insistence, Alexander Hamilton was named inspector general and second in command of the army with the rank of major general. He did not resign from this post until July 2, 1800, nearly two years after his appointment. Congress also enacted a series of internal security measures that included a naturalization act, two laws concerning aliens, and a sedition act. In June, while the alien and sedition acts were progressing through Congress, Jefferson wrote to Madison that "both are so palpably in the teeth of the Constitution as to show they mean to pay no respect to it."[16]

As the presiding officer of the Senate, Vice President Jefferson had to sign the naturalization act and the alien acts, but he left the city before the sedition act could be put before him for his signature. The sedition act made it unlawful for any persons to combine or conspire to oppose any lawful measure of the government, to prevent any officer of the United States from performing his duty, or to aid or attempt to procure any insurrection, riot, or unlawful assembly. It also provided punishment of any person for writing, uttering, or publishing "any false, scandalous and malicious writing" against the president, Congress, or the government of the United States made with the intent to defame or excite against them "the hatred of the good people of the United States." The act was to expire on March 3, 1801, the last day of President Adams's term of office.[17]

Jefferson saw the alien and sedition laws as an attempt to silence Republican newspapers, to drive Republican-minded aliens from the country, and as "an experiment on the American mind to see how far it will bear an avowed violation of the constitution."[18] He soon put his pen to work preparing a series of resolutions against the acts designed to be adopted by some state legislature. He first thought of neighboring North Carolina, but fortuitous circumstances led him to give the resolutions to John Breckinridge, a former Virginian, who was a member of the Kentucky legislature. Breckinridge and members of the Kentucky Assembly toned down Jefferson's words but adopted resolutions that were still strongly worded. Asserting the right of a state to declare an act of Con-

[16] Jefferson to Madison, June 7, 1798, in Smith, ed., *Republic of Letters,* 2 : 1056 – 57.
[17] James Morton Smith, *Freedom's Fetters: The Alien and Sedition Laws and American Civil Liberties* (Ithaca: Cornell University Press, 1956), pp. 94 – 95, 130, 441 – 42.
[18] Jefferson to Stevens T. Mason, Oct. 11, 1798, in Ford, ed., *Jefferson Works,* 8 : 450.

gress unconstitutional and void, the resolutions began with the following resolves.

Kentucky Resolutions of 1798

1. Resolved, that the several states composing the United States of America, are not united on the principle of unlimited submission to their general government; but that by compact under the style and title of a constitution for the United States and of amendments thereto, they constituted a general government for special purposes, delegated to that government certain definitive powers, reserving each state to itself, the residuary mass of right to their own self government; and that whensoever the general government assumes undelegated powers, its acts are unauthoritative, void, and of no force; that to this compact each state acceded, as a state, and is an integral party, its co-states forming as to itself, the other party; that the government created by this compact was not made the exclusive or final *judge* of the extent of the powers delegated to itself; since that would have made its discretion, and not the constitution, the measure of its powers: but that as in all other cases of compact among parties having no common judge, each party has an equal right to judge for itself, as well of infractions as of the mode and measure of redress.

2. Resolved, that the constitution of the United States having delegated to congress a power to punish treason, counterfeiting the securities and current coin of the United States, piracies and felonies committed on the high seas, and offences against the laws of nations, and no other crimes whatever, and it being true as a general principle, and one of the amendments to the constitution having also declared, "that the powers not delegated to the United States by the constitution, nor prohibited by it to the states, are reserved to the states respectively, or to the people," therefore, also the same act of congress passed on the fourteenth day of July, 1798, and entitled "An act in addition to the act entitled an act for the punishment of certain crimes against the United States;" as also the act passed by them on the 27th day of June, 1798, entitled "an act to punish frauds committed on the bank of the United States," (and all other their acts which assume to create, define, or punish crimes other then those enumerated in the constitution) are altogether void and of no force, and that the power to create, define and punish such other crimes is reserved, and

of right appertains solely and exclusively to the respective states, each within its own territory.

3. Resolved, that it is true, as a general principle, and is also expressly declared by one of the amendments to the constitution, that "the powers not delegated to the United States by the constitution, nor prohibited by it to the states, are reserved to the states respectively, or to the people;" and that no power over the freedom of religion, freedom of speech, or freedom of the press being delegated to the United States by the constitution, nor prohibited by it to the states, all lawful powers respecting the same did of right remain, and were reserved to the states, or to the people; that thus was manifested their determination to retain to themselves the right of judging how far the licentiousness of speech and of the press may be abridged, without lessening their useful freedom, and how far those abuses which cannot be separated from their use, should be tolerated, rather than the use be destroyed; and thus also they guarded against all abridgement by the United States of the freedom of religious principles and exercises, and retained to themselves the right of protecting the same, as this state by a law passed on the general demand of its citizens, had already protected them from all human restraint or interference: And that in addition to this general principle and express declaration, another and more special provision has been made by one of the amendments to the constitution, which expressly declares, that "congress shall make no law respecting the establishment of religion, or prohibiting the free exercise thereof, or abridging the freedom of speech, or of the press," thereby guarding in the same sentence, and under the same words, the freedom of religion, of speech, and of the press, insomuch, that whatever violates either, throws down the sanctuary which covers the others, and that libels, falsehoods, and defamation, equally with heresy and false religion, are withheld from the cognizance of federal tribunals. That, therefore, the act of the congress of the United States passed on the fourteenth day of July, 1798, entitled "an act in addition to the act for the punishment of certain crimes against the United States," which does abridge the freedom of the press, is not law, but is altogether void and of no force.

4. Resolved, that alien friends are under the jurisdiction and protection of the laws of the state wherein they are; that no power over them has been delegated to the United States, nor prohibited to the individual states distinct from their power over citizens; and it being true as a general principle, and one of the amendments to the Constitution having also declared, that "the powers not delegated to the United States by the Constitution nor prohibited by it to the states are reserved to the states respectively or to the people," the act of congress of the United States passed on the 22nd day of June, 1798, entitled "an act concerning aliens," which assumes power over alien friends not delegated by the Constitution, is not law, but is altogether void and of no force.

In December 1798, the General Assembly of Virginia also adopted resolutions protesting against the alien and sedition acts. Drafted by James Madison, the resolutions were milder than those adopted in Kentucky but asserted "in case of a deliberate, palpable, and dangerous exercise of other powers not granted" by the Constitution of the United States, the states have the right and the duty to interpose their authority.[19]

In February 1799, Hamilton sent a letter to Theodore Sedgwick, a Federalist senator from Massachusetts, urging him and his colleagues to take action to counteract the Kentucky and Virginia Resolutions.

[19]William T. Hutchinson et al., eds., *The Papers of James Madison,* 17 vols. (Chicago and Charlottesville: University of Virginia Press, 1962–91), 17:189.

ALEXANDER HAMILTON

Letter to Theodore Sedgwick

February 2, 1799

NEW YORK FEBY 2. 1799.

What, My Dear Sir, are you going to do with Virginia? This is a very serious business, which will call for all the wisdom and firmness of the Government. The following are the ideas which occur to me on the occasion.

The first thing in all great operations of such a Government as ours is to secure the opinion of the people. To this end, the proceedings of Virginia and Kentucke with the two laws complained of should be referred to a special Committee. That Committee should make a report exhibiting with great luminousness and particularity the reasons which support the constitutionality and expediency of those laws — the tendency of the doctrines advanced by Virginia and Kentucke to destroy the Constitution of the UStates — and, with calm dignity united with pathos, the full evidence which they afford of a regular conspiracy to overturn the government. And the Report should likewise dwell upon the inevitable effect and probably the intention of these proceedings to encourage a hostile foreign power to decline accommodation and proceed in hostility. The Government must [no]t merely [de]fend itself [bu]t must attack and arraign its enemies. But in all this, there should be great care to distinguish the people of Virginia

Harold C. Syrett et al., eds., *The Papers of Alexander Hamilton,* 27 vols. (New York: Columbia University Press, 1961–87), 22:452–54.

from the legislature and even the greater part of those who may have concurred in the legislature from the Chiefs; manifesting indeed a strong confidence in the good sense and patriotism of the people, that they will not be the dupes of an insidious plan to disunite the people of America to break down their constitution & expose them to the enterprises of a foreign power.

This Report should conclude with a declaration that there is no cause for a Repeal of the laws. If however on examination any modifications consistent with the general design of the laws, but instituting better guards, can be devised it may [be] well to propose them as a bridge for those who may incline to retreat over. Concessions of this kind adroitly made have a good rather than a bad effect. On a recent though hasty revision of the Alien law it seems to me deficient in precautions against abuse and for the security of Citizens. This should not be.

No pains or expence should be spared to dessiminate this Report. A little pamphlet containing it should find its way into every house in Virginia.

This should be left to work and nothing to court a shock should be adopted.

In the mean time the measures for raising the Military force should proceed with activity. Tis much to be lamented that so much delay has attended the execution of this measure. In times like the present not a moment ought to have been lost to secure the Government so powerful an auxiliary. Whenever the experiment shall be made to subdue a *refractory & powerful state* by Militia, the event will shame the advocates of their sufficiency. In the expedition against the Western Insurgents [in Pennsylvania] I trembled every moment lest a great part of the Militia should take it into their heads to return home rather than go forward.

When a clever force has been collected let them be drawn towards Virginia for which there is an obvious pretext — & then let measures be taken to act upon the laws & put Virginia to the Test of resistance.

This plan will give time for the fervour of the moment to subside, for reason to resume the reins, and by dividing its enemies will enable the Government to triumph with ease. . . .

By the fall of 1799, Hamilton was increasingly concerned about the trend of recent events, despite a gain in Federalist members from the South elected to Congress in 1798. As Hamilton looked toward the convening of the Sixth Congress in early December 1799, he wrote a long letter to Jonathan Dayton, a New Jersey Federalist who had been speaker of the House of Representatives in the Third, Fourth, and Fifth Congresses and was now in the Senate.

ALEXANDER HAMILTON

Letter to Jonathan Dayton

[October–November 1799]

[NEW YORK, OCTOBER–NOVEMBER, 1799]
An Accurate view of the internal situation of the UStates presents many
discouraging reflections to the enlightened friends of our Government
and country. Notwithstanding the unexampled success of our public measures at home and abroad — notwithstanding the instructive comments
afforded by the disastrous & disgusting scenes of the french Revolution,
public opinion has not been ameliorated — sentiments dangerous to social happiness have not been diminished — on the contrary there are
symptoms which warrant the apprehension that among the most numerous class of citizens errors of a very pernicious tendency have not only preserved but have extended their empire. Though something may have
been gained on the side of men of information and property, more has
probably been lost on that of persons of different description. An extraordinary exertion of the friends of Government, aided by circumstances of
momentary impression, gave in the last election for members of Congress
a more favourable countenance to some states than they had before
worne. Yet it is the belief of well informed men that no real or desirable
change has been wrought in those States. On the other hand it is admitted
by close observers that some of the parts of the Union which in time past
have been the soundest have of late exhibited signs of a gangrene begun
and progressive.

It is likewise apparent that opposition to the government has acquired
more system than formerly — is bolder in the avowal of its designs — less
solicitous than it was to discriminate between the Constitution and the Administration — more open and more enterprising in its projects.

The late attempt of Virginia & Kentucke to unite the state legislatures
in a direct resistance to certain laws of the Union can be considered in no
other light than as an attempt to change the Government.

It is stated, in addition, that the opposition-Party in Virginia, the head
Quarters of the Faction, have followed up the hostile declarations which
are to be found in the resolutions of their General Assembly by an actual
preparation of the means of supporting them by force — That they have
taken measures to put their militia on a more efficient footing — are preparing considerable arsenals and magazines and (which is an unequivocal

---

Harold C. Syrett et al., eds., *The Papers of Alexander Hamilton,* 27 vols. (New York: Columbia University Press, 1961–87), 23:599–604.

proof how much they are in earnest) have gone so far as to lay new taxes on their citizens.

Amidst such serious indications of hostility, the safety and the duty of the supporters of the Government call upon them to adopt vigorous measures of counteraction. It will be wise in them to act upon the hypothesis that the opposers of the Government are resolved, if it shall be practicable to make its existence a question of force. Possessing as they now do all the constitutional powers, it will be an unpardonable mistake on their part if they do not exert them to surround the constitution with new ramparts and to disconcert the schemes of its enemies.

The measures proper to be adopted may be classed under heads:

1   Establishments which will extend the influence and promote the popularity of the Government.

Under this head three important expedients occur — 1 The Extension of the Judiciary system. 2 The improvement of the great communications as well interiorly as coastwise by turnpike roads. 3 The institution of a Society with funds to be employed in premiums for new inventions discoveries and improvements in Agriculture and in the Arts.

The extension of the Judiciary system ought to embrace two objects — one The subdivision of each state into small Districts (suppose Connecticut into four and so in proportion) assigning to each a Judge with a moderate salary — the other the appointment in each Country of Conservators or Justices of the Peace with only Ministerial functions and with no other compensations than fees for the services they shall perform.

This measure is necessary to give efficacy to the laws the execution of which is obstructed by the want of similar organs and by the indisposition of the local Magistrates in some states. The constitution requires that *Judges* shall have fixed salaries — but this does not apply to mere Justices of the peace without Judicial powers. Both those descriptions of persons are essential as well to the energetic execution of the laws as to the purpose of salutary patronage.

The thing would no doubt be a subject of clamour, but it would carry with it its own antidote, and when once established would bring a very powerful support to the Government.

The improvement of the roads would be a measure universally popular. None can be more so. For this purpose a regular plan should be adopted coextensive with the Union to be successively executed — and a fund should be appropriated sufficient for the basis of a loan of a Milion of Dollars. The revenue of the Post office naturally offers itself. The future revenue from tolls would more than reimburse the expence; and public utility would be promoted in every direction.

The institution of a society with the aid of proper funds to encourage Agriculture and the arts, besides being productive of general advantage, will speak powerfully to the feelings and interests of those classes of men to whom the benefits derived from the Government have been heretofore the least manifest.

2   Provisions for augmenting the means and consolidating the strength of the Government.

A Milion of Dollars may without difficulty be added to the Revenue, by increasing the rates of some existing indirect taxes and by the addition of some new items of a similar character. The direct taxes ought neither to be increased nor diminished.

Our naval force ought to be completed to six Ships of the line Twelve frigates and twenty four sloops of War. More at this juncture would be disproportioned to our resources. Less would be inadequate to the end to be accomplished.

Our Military force should for the present be kept upon its actual footing; making provision for a reinlistment of the men for five years in the event of a settlement of differences with France — with this condition that in case of peace between Great Britain France and Spain, the UStates being then also at peace, all the Privates of twelve additional Regiments of Infantry and of the Regiment of Dragoons exceeding Twenty to a Company shall be disbanded. The corps of Artillerists may be left to retain the numbers which it shall happen to have; but without being recruited until the number of privates shall fall below the standard of the Infantry & Dragoons. A power ought to be given to the President to augment the four Old Regiments to their War Establishmt. . . .

The Institution of a Military Academy will be an auxiliary of great importance.

Manufactories of every article, the woolen parts of cloathing included, which are essential to the supply of the army ought to be established.

3   Arrangements for confirming and enlarging the legal Powers of the Government.

There are several temporary laws which in this view ought to be rendered permanent, particularly that which authorises the calling out of the Militia to suppress unlawful combinations and Insurrections.

An article ought to be proposed to be added to the constitution for empowering Congress to open canals in all cases in which it may be necessary to conduct them through the territory of two or more states or through the territory of a State and that of the UStates. The power is very desireable for the purpose of improving the prodigious facilities for inland navigation with which nature has favoured this Country. It will also assist commerce and agriculture by rendering the transportation of commodities more cheap and expeditious. It will tend to secure the connection by facilitating the communication between distant portions of the Union. And it will be a useful source of influence to the Government.

Happy would it be if a clause would be added to the constitution, enabling Congress on the application of any considerable portion of a state, containing not less than a hundred thousand persons, to erect it into a separate state on the condition of fixing the quota of contributions which it shall make towards antecedent debts, if any there shall be, reserving to Congress the authority to levy within such state the taxes necessary to the payment of such quota, in case of neglect on the part of the State. The subdivision of the great states is indispensable to the security of the General Government and with it of the Union. Great States will always feel a rivalship with the common head, will often be disposed to machinate against it, and in certain situations will be able to do it with decisive effect. The subdivision of such states ought to be a cardinal point in the Fœderal policy: and small states are doubtless best adapted to the purposes of local regulation and to the preservation of the republican spirit. This suggestion however is merely thrown out for consideration. It is feared that it would be inexpedient & even dangerous to propose at this time an amendment of the kind.

4 Laws for restraining and punishing incendiary and seditious practices.

It will be useful to declare that all such writings &c which at common law are libels if levelled against any Officer whatsoever of the UStates shall be cognizable in the Courts of UStates.

To preserve confidence in the Officers of the General Government, by preserving their reputations from malicious and unfounded slanders, is essential to enable them to fulfil the ends of their appointment. It is therefore both constitutional and politic to place their reputations under the guardianship of the Courts of the United States. They ought not to be left to the cold and relucant protection of state courts always temporising sometimes disaffected.

But what avail laws which are not executed? Renegade Aliens conduct more than one of the most incendiary presses in the UStates — and yet in open contempt and defiance of the laws they are permitted to continue their destructive labours. Why are they not sent away? Are laws of this kind passed merely to excite odium and remain a dead letter? Vigour in the Executive is at least as necessary as in the legislative branch. If the President requires to be stimulated those who can approach him ought to do it.

As the presidential election year 1800 approached, Jefferson provided a clear expression of his political views in correspondence with friends. One of his most important statements can be found in a letter to Elbridge Gerry of Massachusetts, a signer of the Declaration of Independence, a delegate to the Constitutional Convention, and a former member of Congress. Most recently, Gerry had been on a diplomatic mission to France.

In writing to Gerry, Jefferson succinctly affirmed the basic political beliefs to which he could be expected to adhere in the approaching contest and as president.

THOMAS JEFFERSON

Letter to Elbridge Gerry

January 26, 1799

. . . I do then, with sincere zeal, wish an inviolable preservation of our present federal constitution, according to the true sense in which it was adopted by the States, that in which it was advocated by it's friends, & not that which it's enemies apprehended, who therefore became it's enemies; and I am opposed to the monarchising it's features by the forms of it's administration, with a view to conciliate a first transition to a President & Senate for life, & from that to a hereditary tenure of these offices, & thus to worm out the elective principle. I am for preserving to the States the powers not yielded by them to the Union, & to the legislature of the Union it's constitutional share in the division of powers; and I am not for transferring all the powers of the States to the general government, & all those of that government to the Executive branch. I am for a government rigorously frugal & simple, applying all the possible savings of the public revenue to the discharge of the national debt; and not for a multiplication of officers & salaries merely to make partisans, & for increasing, by every device, the public debt, on the principle of it's being a public blessing. I am for relying, for internal defence, on our militia solely, till actual invasion, and for such a naval force only as may protect our coasts and harbors from such depredations as we have experienced; and not for a standing army in time of peace, which may overawe the public sentiment; nor for a navy, which, by it's own expenses and the eternal wars in which it will implicate us, grind us with public burthens, & sink us under them. I am for free commerce with all nations; political connection with none; & little or no diplomatic establishment. And I am not for linking ourselves by new treaties with the quarrels of Europe; entering that field of slaughter to preserve their balance, or joining in the confederacy of kings to war against the principles of liberty. I am for freedom of religion, & against all maneuvres to bring about a legal ascendancy of one sect over another: for freedom of

Paul L. Ford, ed., *The Works of Thomas Jefferson,* Federal Edition, 12 vols. (New York: G. P. Putnam's Sons, 1904), 9:17–19.

Figure 6. *The Providential Detection.*

The artist depicts Jefferson as an unwavering friend of France, kneeling before the "Altar to Gallic Despotism" and being prevented by a divinely directed American eagle from sacrificing the Constitution of the United States and American independence. A controversial letter to Philip Mazzei, a friend in Italy, falls from Jefferson's right hand. That letter, in which Jefferson denounced "an Anglican monarchical and aristicratical" party in the United States, was published in Florence and in Paris and reprinted in Philadelphia in the *Gazette of the United States* on May 4, 1797.

Library Company of Philadelphia.

the press, & against all violations of the constitution to silence by force & not by reason the complaints or criticisms, just or unjust, of our citizens against the conduct of their agents. And I am for encouraging the progress of science in all it's branches; and not for raising a hue and cry against the sacred name of philosophy; for awing the human mind by stories of raw-head & bloody bones to a distrust of its own vision, & to repose implicitly on that of others; to go backwards instead of forwards to look for improvement; to believe that government, religion, morality, & every other science were in the highest perfection in ages of the darkest ignorance, and that nothing can ever be devised more perfect than what was established by our forefathers. To these I will add, that I was a sincere well-wisher to the success of the French revolution, and still wish it may end in the establishment of a free & well-ordered republic; but I have not been insensible under the atrocious depredations they have committed on our commerce. The first object of my heart is my own country. In that is embarked my family, my fortune, & my own existence. I have not one farthing of interest, nor one fibre of attachment out of it, nor a single motive of preference of any one nation to another, but in proportion as they are more or less friendly to us. But though deeply feeling the injuries of France, I did not think war the surest means of redressing them. I did believe, that a mission sincerely disposed to preserve peace, would obtain for us a peaceable & honorable settlement & retribution; and I appeal to you to say, whether this might not have been obtained, if either of your colleagues had been of the same sentiment with yourself.

These, my friend, are my principles; they are unquestionably the principles of the great body of our fellow citizens. . . .

No more succinct and elegant summation of Jefferson's basic political views can be found than in the preceding letter to a New England political friend. As the eighteenth century drew to a close, Thomas Jefferson and Alexander Hamilton, more clearly than any other two American statesmen, represented the diverging views and positions of the developing national political parties coalescing under the banners of Federalist and Republican.

6

Political Competitors

In 1800, Thomas Jefferson and Alexander Hamilton were prominent competitors for political support, but in very different roles. Vice President Jefferson was a candidate for president of the United States, nominated by Republican members of Congress in a party caucus. Hamilton, not being a native-born American, could never be a candidate for president, but he would play an active role in the election of candidates for that high post. As a leading New York Federalist, Hamilton directed the political campaign in New York City in opposition to Jefferson, whose supporters were led by Aaron Burr. Because presidential electors in New York in 1800 were chosen by the state legislature, the election of members of the legislature would determine the state's electoral vote.

In the presidential election in 1796, the New York vote had been cast for John Adams. In 1800, Republicans saw the contest as an uphill struggle because in the previous New York legislative election of 1798, the Federalists had won all the seats from New York City. In that election, it was reported that "Hamilton has attended, in company with other leaders of his party, *all* the polls of this city, *daily* and *hourly*." [1]

In the contest for the New York state assembly in 1800, Burr and Hamilton and their lieutenants were equally active. "The election was extremely warm and contested," reported one Hamiltonian aide. "Never have I witnessed such exertions on either side before." [2] Hamilton's efforts, however, failed to bring a Federalist victory. When the polls closed and the votes were counted, the Republican candidates in New York City had won all thirteen contests for legislative seats. At midnight on May 1, 1800, Matthew L. Davis, an active Republican worker, jubilantly wrote

[1] Matthew L. Davis to Albert Gallatin, Apr. 26, 1798, Albert Gallatin Papers, New-York Historical Society.
[2] Robert Troup to Peter Van Schaack, May 2, 1800, Peter Van Schaack Papers, Library of Congress.

128

across the top of a letter to Congressman Albert Gallatin of Pennsylvania, "Republicanism Triumphant. To Col. Burr we are indebted for every thing."[3]

On Saturday morning, May 3, 1800, the news of the New York election reached the capital in Philadelphia. Exuberant Republican congressmen immediately commissioned Gallatin to obtain information from New York Republicans regarding their favored candidate for the vice presidential nomination. After Gallatin reported that Burr was the choice of New York leaders, Republicans in Congress caucused on May 10 and unanimously agreed to support Burr for vice president.[4] Although the understanding was that Burr was the candidate for vice president, there was no separate balloting for president and vice president before the adoption of the Twelfth Amendment in 1804. At this time, each presidential elector cast two votes without distinguishing between president and vice president. The candidate receiving the largest number of votes — provided it constituted a majority of the votes cast — became president. The candidate with the next highest number of votes became vice president.

While Republicans celebrated their victory in New York, Federalists despaired. On May 4, Hamilton wrote to Theodore Sedgwick, Speaker of the House of Representatives, urging that Charles Cotesworth Pinckney of South Carolina be supported equally with John Adams.

[3] Davis to Gallatin, Thursday night, 12 o'clock, May 1, 1800, Gallatin Papers, New-York Historical Society.

[4] Noble E. Cunningham Jr., "Election of 1800," in Arthur M. Schlesinger Jr., ed., *The Coming to Power: Critical Elections in American History* (New York: Chelsea House and McGraw-Hill, 1972), p. 42.

Figure 7. (opposite) *Engraving of Thomas Jefferson, by Cornelius Tiebout.*
In this engraving, published by Augustus Day in Philadelphia on July 4, 1801, Jefferson is pictured holding the Declaration of Independence and surrounded by things that described and interested him. A table to his right holds books and a bust of Benjamin Franklin, and on his left a static electrical machine indicates Jefferson's interest in science. Jefferson's image was taken from a bust portrait painted by Rembrandt Peale.
Library of Congress, Prints and Photographs Division.

ALEXANDER HAMILTON

Letter to Theodore Sedgwick

May 4, 1800

You have heard of the loss of our Election in the City of New York. This renders it too probable that the Electors of President in this State will be Antifederal. If so, the policy I was desirous of pursuing at the last Election is now recommended by motives of additional urgency. To support *Adams and Pinckney,* equally, is the only thing that can possibly save us from the fangs of *Jefferson.*

It is therefore essential that the Federalists should not separate without coming to a distinct and solemn concert to pursue this course *bona fide.*

Pray attend to this and let me speedily hear from you that it is done.

Hamilton's Federalist friends in Congress did not wait for advice from New York before acting. On the evening of May 3 — the day that the news of the New York election reached Philadelphia — Federalists in Congress gathered in a party caucus and agreed to support Adams and Charles Cotesworth Pinckney, of South Carolina, equally as candidates for president.[5] Like Hamilton, anti-Adams Federalists in Congress hoped that in the event of a tie between Adams and Pinckney — sending the election to be decided by the House of Representatives — some Republicans might vote for Pinckney and elect him president.

Soon after the New York election, Hamilton wrote directly to New York governor John Jay, a fellow Federalist, urging him to call a special session of the current, Federalist-controlled legislature. The aim would be to change the state laws to provide for a district system of popular election of presidential electors instead of electors being chosen by the legislature.[6]

---

[5] Theodore Sedgwick to Rufus King, May 11, 1800, in Charles R. King, ed., *The Life and Correspondence of Rufus King,* 6 vols. (New York: G. P. Putnam's Sons, 1894–1900), 3:238.

[6] At the time Hamilton wrote this letter, the Pennsylvania legislature had adjourned without passing an election law, and it appeared that no state vote would be cast. Later, however, an election law was enacted.

Harold C. Syrett et al., eds., *The Papers of Alexander Hamilton,* 27 vols. (New York: Columbia University Press, 1960–87), 24:452–53.

ALEXANDER HAMILTON

Letter to John Jay

May 7, 1800

Dear Sir:

You have been informed of the loss of our Election in this City. It is also known that we have been unfortunate throughout Long Island & in West Chester. According to the Returns hitherto, it is too probable that we lose our Senators for this District.

The moral certainty therefore is that there will be an Anti-fœderal Majority in the Ensuing Legislature, and this very high probability is that this will bring *Jefferson* into the Chief Magistracy; unless it be prevented by the measure which I shall now submit to your consideration, namely the immediate calling together of the existing Legislature.

I am aware that there are weighty objections to the measure; but the reasons for it appear to me to outweigh the objections. And in times like these in which we live, it will not do to be overscrupulous. It is easy to sacrifice the substantial interests of society by a strict adherence to ordinary rules.

In observing this, I shall not be supposed to mean that any thing ought to be done which integrity will forbid — but merely that the scruples of delicacy and propriety, as relative to a common course of things, ought to yield to the extraordinary nature of the crisis. They ought not to hinder the taking of a *legal* and *constitutional* step, to prevent an *Atheist* in Religion and a *Fanatic* in politics from getting possession of the helm of the State.

You Sir know in a great degree the Antifœderal party, but I fear that you do not know them as well as I do. Tis a composition indeed of very incongruous materials but all tending to mischief — some of them to the overthrow of the Government by stripping it of its due energies others of them to a Revolution after the manner of Buonaparte. I speak from indubitable facts, not from conjectures & inferences.

In proportion as the true character of this party is understood is the force of the considerations which urge to every effort to disappoint it. And it seems to me that there is a very solemn obligation to employ the means in our power.

The calling of the Legislature will have for object the choosing of Electors by the people in Districts. This (as Pennsylvania will do nothing) will insure a Majority of votes in the U States for Fœderal Candidates.

Harold C. Syrett et al., eds., *The Papers of Alexander Hamilton,* 27 vols. (New York: Columbia University Press, 1960–87), 24:464–66.

The measure will not fail to be approved by all the Fœderal Party; while it will no doubt be condemned by the opposite. As to its intrinsic nature it is justified by unequivocal reasons for *public safety.*

The reasonable part of the world will I believe approve it. They will see it as a proceeding out of the common course but warranted by the particular nature of the Crisis and the great cause of social order.

If done the motive ought to be frankly avowed. In your communication to the Legislature they ought to be told that Temporary circumstances had rendered it probable that without their interposition the executive authority of the General Government would be transfered to hands hostile to the system heretofore pursued with so much success and dangerous to the peace happiness and order of the Country — that under this impression from facts convincing to your own mind you had thought it your duty to give the existing Legislature an opportunity of deliberating whether it would not be proper to interpose and endeavour to prevent so great an evil by referring the choice of Electors to the People distributed into Districts.

In weighing this suggestion you will doubtless bear in mind that Popular Governments must certainly be overturned & while they endure prove engines of mischief — if one party will call to its aid all the resources which *Vice* can give and if the other, however pressing the emergency, confines itself within all the ordinary forms of delicacy and decorum.

The legislature can be brought together in three weeks. So that there will be full time for the objects; but none ought to be lost.

Think well my Dear Sir of this proposition. Appreciate the extreme danger of the Crisis; and I am unusually mistaken in my view of the matter, if you do not see it right and expedient to adopt the measure.

Respectfully & Affecty   Yrs.   A HAMILTON

Governor Jay immediately rejected Hamilton's advice, writing at the bottom of Hamilton's letter, "Proposing a measure for party purposes which I think it would not become me to adopt."[7] As the campaign of 1800 progressed, Hamilton began urging friends in states where Federalists were strong to seek Federalist electors who would vote only for Pinckney. Before the contest was over, Hamilton broke openly with Adams. In a *Letter from Alexander Hamilton, Concerning the Public Conduct and Character of John Adams, Esq., President of the United States,* Hamilton attacked Adams directly. The letter, however, appeared too

[7]Hamilton to Jay, May 7, 1800, in Harold C. Syrett et al., eds., *The Papers of Alexander Hamilton,* 27 vols. (New York: Columbia University Press, 1960–87), 24:467.

late in the campaign to provide much help to the Republicans. When the electoral vote was counted, the result was Jefferson 73, Burr 73, Adams 65, Pinckney 64, and John Jay 1.

Hamilton's scheme had failed, and the Federalists had withheld one vote from Pinckney. The Republican supporters of Jefferson, however, had not guarded against a tie vote between Jefferson and Burr. "The Feds in the legislature have expressed dispositions to make all they can of the embarrassment," Jefferson wrote to James Monroe, "so that after the most energetic efforts, crowned with success, we remain in the hands of our enemies by the want of foresight in the original arrangements."[8]

Before the electoral vote was officially counted, the outcome had been anticipated from various reports coming from different states. In mid-December 1800, Hamilton wrote from New York to Oliver Wolcott Jr., his successor as secretary of the Treasury,

> It is now, my Dear Sir, ascertained that Jefferson or Burr will be President and it seems probable that they will come with equal votes to the House of Representatives. It is also circulated here that in this event the Federalists in Congress or some of them talk of preferring Burr. I trust New England at least will not so far lose its head as to fall into this snare. There is no doubt but that upon every virtuous and prudent calculation Jefferson is to be preferred. He is by far not so dangerous a man and he has pretensions to character.[9]

In the election in the House of Representatives to decide the electoral tie between Jefferson and Burr, voting was by states, each state casting one vote. Although the Federalists had a majority in the House, neither party controlled a majority of the state delegations. Two state delegations (Maryland and Vermont) were equally divided, and Republicans needed the vote of one of these states to elect Jefferson. From the outset, Alexander Hamilton urged Federalists in the House to support Jefferson rather than Burr, but his advice was ignored.

In the weeks preceding the House's balloting to decide the tie vote between Jefferson and Burr, Hamilton wrote numerous letters to Federalist friends condemning Burr as unfit for the high office and presenting arguments in favor of Jefferson. Delaware's sole Congressman, Federalist James A. Bayard, who would cast that state's vote, was subjected to

[8] Jefferson to James Monroe, Dec. 20, 1800, James Monroe Papers, Library of Congress.
[9] Hamilton to Wolcott, Dec. 16, 1800, in Syrett et al., eds., *Hamilton Papers,* 25:257.

particular pressure from Hamilton. In letters to Bayard arguing Burr's unfitness for office, Hamilton displayed his complete contempt for Burr. He also assessed Jefferson's strengths and weaknesses.

ALEXANDER HAMILTON
Letter to James A. Bayard
December 27, 1800

NEW-YORK DECEMBER. 27TH. 1800.
Dear Sir:
Several letters to myself & others from the City of Washington, excite in my mind extreme alarm on the subject of the future President. It seems nearly ascertained that *Jefferson & Burr* will come into the house of Rs. with equal votes, and those letters express the probability that the Fœderal Party may prefer the latter. In my opinion a circumstance more ruinous to them, or more disastrous to the Country could not happen. This opinion is dictated by a long & close attention to the character, with the best opportunities of knowing it; an advant[ag]e for judging which few of our friends possess, & which ought to give some weight to my opinion. Be assured my dear Sir, that this man has no principle public or private. As a politician his sole spring of action is an inordinate ambition; as an individual he is believed by friends as well as foes to be without *probity,* and a voluptuary by system, with habits of expence that can be satisfied by no fair expedients. As to his talents, great management & cunning are the predominant features — he is yet to give proofs of those solid abilities which characterize the statesman. Daring & energy must be allowed him but these qualities under the direction of the worst passions, are certainly strong objections not recommendations. He is of a temper to undertake the most hazadrous enterprizes because he is sanguine enough to think nothing impracticable, and of an ambition which will be content with nothing less than *permanent* power in his own hands. The maintenance of the existing institutions will not suit him, because under them his power will be too narrow & too precarious; yet the innovations he may attempt will not offer the substitute of a system *durable & safe,* calculated to give lasting prosperity, & to unite liberty with strength. It will be the system of the day, sufficient to serve his own turn, & not looking beyond himself. To ex-

Harold C. Syrett et al., eds., *The Papers of Alexander Hamilton,* 27 vols. (New York: Columbia University Press, 1961–87), 25:275–77.

ecute this plan as the good men of the country cannot be relied upon, the worst will be used. Let it not be imagined that the difficulties of execution will deter, or a calculation of interest restrain. The truth is that under forms of Government like ours, too much is practicable to men who will without scruple avail themselves of the bad passions of human nature. To a man of this description possessing the requisite talents, the acquisition of permanent power is not a Chimæra. I *know* that Mr Burr does not view it as such, & I am sure there are no means too atrocious to be employed by him. In debt vastly beyond his means of payment, with all the habits of excessive expence, he cannot be satisfied with the regular emoluments of any office of our Government. Corrupt expedients will be to him a *necessary* resource. Will any prudent man offer such a president to the temptations of foreign gold? No engagement that can be made with him can be depended upon. While making it he will laugh in his sleeve at the credulity of those with whom he makes it — and the first moment it suits his views to break it he will do so. Let me add that I could scarcely name a discreet man of either party in our State, who does not think Mr Burr the most unfit man in the U.S. for the office of President. Disgrace abroad ruin at home are the probable fruits of his elevation. To contribute to the disappointment and mortification of Mr J. would be on my part, only to retaliate for unequivocal proofs of enmity; but in a case like this it would be base to listen to personal considerations. In alluding to the situation I mean only to illustrate how strong must be the motives which induce me to promote *his* elevation in exclusion of another. For Heaven's sake my dear Sir, exert yourself to the utmost to save our country from so great a calamity. Let us not be responsible for the evils which in all probability will follow the preference. All calculations that may lead to it must prove fallacious.

ALEXANDER HAMILTON

Letter to James A. Bayard

January 16, 1801

. . . Perhaps myself the first, at some expence of popularity, to unfold the true character of Jefferson, it is too late for me to become his apologist. Nor can I have any disposition to do it. I admit that his politics are tinctured

Harold C. Syrett et al., eds., *The Papers of Alexander Hamilton,* 27 vols. (New York: Columbia University Press, 1961–87), 25:319–20.

with fanaticism, that he is too much in earnest in his democracy, that he has been a mischevous enemy to the principle measures of our past administration, that he is crafty & persevering in his objects, that he is not scrupulous about the means of success, nor very mindful of truth, and that he is a contemptible hypocrite. But it is not true as is alleged that he is an enemy to the power of the Executive, or that he is for confounding all the powers in the House of Rs. It is a fact which I have frequently mentioned that while we were in the administration together he was generally for a large construction of the Executive authority, & not backward to act upon it in cases which coincided with his views. Let it be added, that in his theoretic Ideas he has considered as improper the participations of the Senate in the Executive Authority. I have more than once made the reflection that viewing himself as the reversioner, he was solicitous to come into possession of a Good Estate. Nor is it true that Jefferson is zealot enough to do anything in pursuance of his principles which will contravene his popularity, or his interest. He is as likely as any man I know to temporize — to calculate what will be likely to promote his own reputation and advantage; and the probable result of such a temper is the preservation of systems, though originally opposed, which being once established, could not be overturned without danger to the person who did it. To my mind a true estimate of Mr J.'s character warrants the expectation of a temporizing rather than violent system. . . .

When balloting began in the House of Representatives on February 11, 1801, Federalists did not follow Hamilton's advice to vote for Jefferson rather than Burr. On the first ballot the vote was eight states for Jefferson (New York, New Jersey, Pennsylvania, Virginia, North Carolina, Georgia, Kentucky, and Tennessee); six states for Burr (New Hampshire, Massachusetts, Rhode Island, Connecticut, Delaware, and South Carolina); and two states divided (Vermont and Maryland). On February 17, after nearly a week of balloting repeatedly produced the same result, the deadlock was broken on the thirty-sixth ballot. Vermont and Maryland joined the eight states that had voted for Jefferson, electing him the third president of the United States. On this final ballot — in which Bayard was a key figure in the decision to concede to Jefferson's election — Delaware cast a blank ballot. Federalist representatives from Maryland and Vermont either did not vote or cast blank ballots. Only New Hampshire, Massachusetts, Rhode Island, and Connecticut voted for Burr.

As Hamilton continued *The Examination,* his pieces became more verbose. Midway through the critique, Hamilton paused to review some of his leading arguments. No longer in public office or military service, Hamilton retained his deep interest in public affairs, but his own prominence in the public eye had diminished. Although Hamilton's close connections with the *New-York Evening Post* must have led many informed readers to conclude that "Lucius Crassus" was Alexander Hamilton, the pieces did not attract any major reply, and they have not received much attention from historians.[9]

[9] A major exception is Harvey Flaumenhaft, who devotes a chapter to the articles in *The Effective Republic: Administration and Constitution in the Thought of Alexander Hamilton* (Durham, N.C.: Duke University Press, 1992), pp. 225–49.

ALEXANDER HAMILTON

The Examination, Number IX

January 18, 1802

[NEW YORK, JANUARY 18, 1802]
The leading points of the Message have been sufficiently canvassed, and it is believed to have been fully demonstrated, that this communication is chargeable with all the faults which were imputed to it on the outset of the Examination. We have shewn that it has made or attempted to make prodigal sacrifices of constitutional energy, of sound principle, and of public interest. In the doctrine respecting war, there is a senseless abandonment of the just and necessary authority of the Executive Department, in a point material to our national safety. In the proposals to relinquish the internal revenue, there is an attempt to establish a precedent ruinous to our public credit; calculated to prolong the burthen of the debt, and generally to enfeeble and sink the government, by depriving it of resources of great importance to its respectability, to the accomplishment of its most salutary plans, to its power of being useful. In the attack upon the judiciary establishment, there is a plain effort to impair that organ of the government; one on which its efficiency and success absolutely depend. In the recommendation to admit indiscriminately foreign emigrants of every description to the privileges of American citizens, on their first entrance into our coun-

Harold C. Syrett et al., eds., *The Papers of Alexander Hamilton,* 27 vols. (New York: Columbia University Press, 1961–87), 25:500–4.

With only two weeks to prepare for his inauguration, President-Elect Jefferson concentrated on drafting his inaugural address. He was at no loss as to what to say, for as the election campaign had approached he had reiterated in private letters his basic political beliefs and the policies that would guide his actions as president. His challenge now was to re-affirm those beliefs and principles in words that would be long remembered. Through three drafts, Jefferson revised and polished his address until he had composed a succinct and eloquent summation of his basic beliefs and the principles that would direct his policies and actions as president of the United States. His carefully chosen words and the deeply believed principles upon which the address rested destined it to become one of the memorable inaugural addresses in American history.

THOMAS JEFFERSON

Inaugural Address

March 4, 1801

Friends and fellow citizens:
Called upon to undertake the duties of the first Executive office of our country, I avail myself of the presence of that portion of my fellow citizens which is here assembled to express my grateful thanks for the favor with which they have been pleased to look towards me, to declare a sincere consciousness that the task is above my talents, and that I approach it with those anxious and awful presentiments which the greatness of the charge, and the weakness of my powers so justly inspire. A rising nation, spread over a wide and fruitful land, traversing all the seas with the rich productions of their industry, engaged in commerce with nations who feel power and forget right, advancing rapidly to destinies beyond the reach of mortal eye, when I contemplate these transcendent objects, and see the honour, the happiness, and the hopes of this beloved country committed to the issue and the auspices of this day, I shrink from the contemplation, and humble myself before the magnitude of the undertaking. Utterly indeed should I despair, did not the presence of many, whom I here

Thomas Jefferson, Inaugural Address, Mar. 4, 1801, manuscript sent to Samuel Harrison Smith for publication in the *National Intelligencer,* Thomas Jefferson Papers, Library of Congress.

Figure 8. *View of the Capitol, Washington, D.C., Watercolor by William Birch, 1800.*
Shown is the Senate wing of the unfinished Capitol where, in the Senate chamber, Jefferson took the oath of office as president of the United States and delivered his inaugural address on March 4, 1801.
Library of Congress, Prints and Photographs Division.

see, remind me, that, in the other high authorities provided by our constitution, I shall find resources of wisdom, of virtue, and of zeal, on which to rely under all difficulties. To you, then, gentlemen, who are charged with the sovereign functions of legislation, and to those associated with you, I look with encouragement for that guidance and support which may enable us to steer with safety the vessel in which we are all embarked, amidst the conflicting elements of a troubled world.

During the contest of opinion through which we have past, the animation of discussions and of exertions has sometimes worn an aspect which might impose on strangers unused to think freely, and to speak and to write what they think. But this being now decided by the voice of the nation, enounced according to the rules of the constitution, all will of course arrange themselves under the will of the law, and unite in common efforts for the common good. All too will bear in mind this sacred principle that though the will of the majority is in all cases to prevail, that will, to be rightful, must be reasonable; that the minority possess their equal rights, which equal laws must protect and to violate would be oppression. Let us then fellow citizens unite with one heart and one mind, let us restore to social intercourse that harmony and affection without which liberty, and even life itself, are but dreary things. And let us reflect that having banished from our land that religious intolerance under which mankind so long bled and suffered, we have yet gained little if we countenance a political intolerance, as despotic, as wicked, and capable of as bitter and bloody persecutions. During the throes and convulsions of the ancient world, during the agonizing spasms of infuriated man, seeking through blood and slaughter his long-lost liberty, it was not wonderful that the agitation of the billows should reach even this distant and peaceful shore; that this should be more felt and feared by some and less by others; and should divide opinions as to measures of safety. But every difference of opinion is not a difference of principle. We have called by different names brethren of the same principle. We are all republicans: we are all federalists. If there be any among us who would wish to dissolve this Union or to change it's republican form, let them stand undisturbed as monuments of the safety with which error of opinion may be tolerated, where reason is left free to combat it. I know indeed that some honest men fear that a republican government cannot be strong, that this government is not strong enough. But would the honest patriot in the full tide of successful experiment abandon a government which has so far kept us free and firm, on the theoretic and visionary fear, that this government, the world's best hope, may, by possibility, want energy to preserve itself? I trust not, I believe this, on the contrary, the strongest government on earth. I believe it the only one, where every man, at the call of the law, would fly to the standard of the law, and would meet invasions of the public order as his own personal concern. Sometimes it is said that man cannot be trusted with the government of himself. Can he then be trusted with the government of others? Or have we found angels, in the form of kings, to govern him? Let history answer this question.

Let us then, with courage and confidence, pursue our own federal and republican principles; our attachments to union and representative government. Kindly separated by nature and a wide ocean from the exterminating havoc of one quarter of the globe; too high-minded to endure the degradations of the others, possessing a chosen country, with room enough for our descendants to the thousandth and thousandth generation, entertaining a due sense of our equal right to use of our own faculties, to the acquisitions of our own industry, to honour and confidence from our fellow citizens, resulting not from birth, but from our actions and their sense of them, enlightened by a benign religion, professed indeed and practised in various forms, yet all of them inculcating Honesty,

truth, temperance, gratitude and the love of man, acknoleging and ador-
ing an overruling providence, which by it's dispensations proves that it de-
lights in the happiness of man here, and his greater happiness hereafter;
with all these blessings, what more is necessary to make us a happy and
prosperous people? Still one thing more fellow citizens, a wise and frugal
government which shall restrain men from injuring one another, shall
leave them otherwise free to regulate their own pursuits of industry and
improvement, and shall not take from the mouth of labor the bread it has
earned. This is the sum of good government; and this is necessary to close
the circle of our felicities.

About to enter, fellow citizens, on the exercise of duties which com-
prehend every thing dear and valuable to you, it is proper you should understand what I deem the essential principles of our government and consequently those which ought to shape it's administration. I will compress
them within the narrowest compass they will bear, stating the general
principle, but not all it's limitations. — Equal and exact justice to all men,
of whatever state or persuasion, religious or political: — Peace, commerce
and honest friendship with all nations, entangling alliances with none:
— the support of the state governments in all their rights as the most
competent administrations for our domestic concerns, and the surest
bulwarks against anti-republican tendencies: — the preservation of the
General government in it's whole constitutional vigour as the sheet anchor
of our peace at home, and safety abroad: — a jealous care of the right of
election by the people, a mild and safe corrective of abuses which are
lopped by the sword or revolution where peaceable remedies are unpro-
vided: — absolute acquiescence in the decisions of the majority, the vital
principle of republics, from which is no appeal but to force, the vital principle and immediate parent of despotism: — a well disciplined militia, our
best reliance in peace, and for the first moments of war, till regulars may
relieve them: — the supremacy of the civil over the military authority; —
economy in the Public expence, that labor may be lightly burthened: —
the honest payment of our debts and sacred preservation of the public
faith: — encouragement of agriculture, and of commerce as it's hand-
maid: — the diffusion of information, and the arraignment of all abuses at
the bar of the public reason: — freedom of religion; freedom of the press;
and freedom of person, under the protection of Habeas corpus: — and trial
by juries, impartially selected. These principles form the bright constella-
tion, which has gone before us and guided our steps through an age of revolution and reformation. The wisdom of our sages and blood of our heroes
have been devoted to their attainment: they should be the creed of our political faith, the text of civic instruction, the touchstone by which to try the
services of those we trust. And should we wander from them in moments
of error or of alarm, let us hasten to retrace our steps, and to regain the
road which alone leads to Peace, liberty and safety.

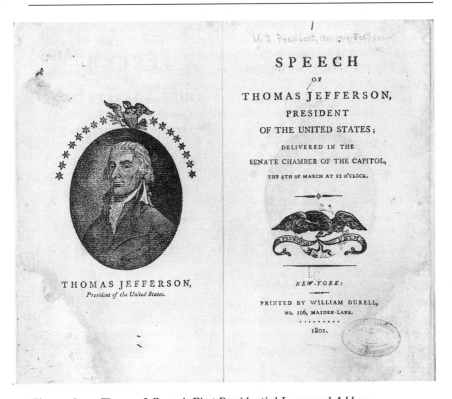

Figure 9. *Thomas Jefferson's First Presidential Inaugural Address.*
Printed by William Durell, New York, 1801. Frontispiece and title page. Engraving by unknown artist.
Rare Books and Special Collections Division, Library of Congress.

I repair then, fellow citizens, to the post you have assigned me. With experience enough in subordinate offices to have seen the difficulties of this the greatest of all, I have learnt to expect that it will rarely fall to the lot of imperfect man to retire from this station with the reputation, and the favor, which bring him into it. Without pretensions to that high confidence you reposed in our first and greatest revolutionary character, whose preeminent services had entitled him to the first place in his country's love — and destined for him the fairest page in the volume of faithful history, I ask so much confidence only as may give firmness and effect to the legal administration of your affairs. I shall often go wrong through defect of judgment. When right, I shall often be thought wrong by those whose positions will not command a view of the whole ground. I ask your indulgence for my own errors, which will never be intentional; and your support against the errors of others, who may condemn what they would not, if seen in all it's parts. The approbation implied by your suffrage is a great consolation to me for the past; and my future solicitude will be to retain the good opinion of those who have bestowed it in advance, to conciliate that of others by doing them all the good in my power, and to be instrumental to the happiness and freedom of all.

Relying then on the patronage of your good will, I advance with obedience to the work ready to retire from it whenever you become sensible how much better choices it is in your power to make. And may that infinite power which rules the destinies of the universe lead our councils to what is best, and give them a favourable issue for your peace and prosperity.

7

Hamilton and President Jefferson

In an address on March 21, 1801, to the voters of New York during the state gubernatorial election, Alexander Hamilton said in reference to President Thomas Jefferson's recent inaugural address of March 4, "We think it proper to make a public declaration of our approbation of its contents: We view it as virtually a candid retraction of past misapprehensions, and a pledge to the community that the new President will not lend himself to dangerous innovations, but in essential points will tread in the steps of his predecessors."[1]

A few weeks later, however, in a speech at a Federalist Party meeting in New York City, Hamilton left a quite different impression. He said that he considered only two things "positively pledged" by Jefferson's speech: freedom from alliances and the preservation of credit. "Although these were very important objects and if secured would redound much to his honor," one listener recorded him as saying, "yet he considered him as being wholly silent on several other points of great moment." This reporter also recorded Hamilton as contrasting President Jefferson's conduct since taking office with the professions of his inaugural address and suggesting that "if they were made with sincerity he had not firmness enough to adhere to them."[2] By the time Jefferson sent his first annual address to Congress in December 1801, Hamilton's criticism of the new president had become sharp and extensive.

Long before he drafted his first annual address to Congress, Jefferson

---

[1] Alexander Hamilton, An Address to the Electors of the State of New York, [Mar. 21, 1801], in Harold C. Syrett et al., eds., *The Papers of Alexander Hamilton,* 27 vols. (New York: Columbia University Press, 1961–87), 25:365.

[2] Alexander Hamilton, campaign speech, [New York, April 10, 1801], as reported by Robert Troup in a letter to Rufus King, May 27, 1801, ibid., p. 377.

had decided that he would send a written message rather than deliver an address in person, as had been done by Presidents Washington and Adams. To Jefferson and other Republicans, an address to Congress by the president in person too closely resembled the address to Parliament by the British monarch.

Jefferson devoted considerable time and effort to preparing his first annual message to Congress, and he involved the members of his cabinet in the process. Four weeks before sending it to Congress, Jefferson circulated a draft among the department heads and revised it in response to their suggestions.[3] Jefferson's message proposed the specific implementation of many of the policy objectives he had put forward during the campaign of 1800 and had reiterated in his inaugural address. He recommended abolishing all internal taxes, including the tax on whiskey, and reducing the army, the navy, and the civil establishment. He proposed revising the judiciary structure and militia laws and reducing the residence requirements for naturalization.

Early in his message, Jefferson addressed the recent naval confrontation in the Mediterranean Sea with the Barbary pirates. As secretary of state, Jefferson had favored having a naval force in the Mediterranean to protect American commerce, but Congress had chosen to continue paying tribute and ransom to protect American commerce. As one of his first problems as president, Jefferson faced reports that Tripoli had sent cruisers to attack American shipping in the Mediterranean. With the approval and support of his cabinet, Jefferson sent a squadron to the Mediterranean Sea. In his message, he reported and defended the military action, which had taken place without a declaration of war.

On December 8, 1801, Meriwether Lewis, Jefferson's private secretary, carried the president's message to both houses of Congress.

---

[3] Jefferson to Madison, Nov. 12, 1801, Jefferson to Gallatin, Nov. 14, 1801, in Paul L. Ford, ed., *The Works of Thomas Jefferson,* Federal Edition, 12 vols. (New York: G. P. Putnam's Sons, 1904), 9:321–22; Noble E. Cunningham Jr., *The Process of Government under Jefferson* (Princeton: Princeton University Press, 1978), pp. 72–77.

First Annual Message to Congress

December 8, 1801

DECEMBER 8, 1801.

Fellow Citizens of the Senate and House of Representatives:

It is a circumstance of sincere gratification to me that on meeting the great council of our nation, I am able to announce to them, on the grounds of reasonable certainty, that the wars and troubles which have for so many years afflicted our sister nations have at length come to an end, and that the communications of peace and commerce are once more opening among them. While we devoutly return thanks to the beneficent Being who has been pleased to breathe into them the spirit of conciliation and forgiveness, we are bound with peculiar gratitude to be thankful to him that our own peace has been preserved through so perilous a season, and ourselves permitted quietly to cultivate the earth and to practice and improve those arts which tend to increase our comforts. The assurances, indeed, of friendly disposition, received from all the powers with whom we have principal relations, had inspired a confidence that our peace with them would not have been disturbed. But a cessation of the irregularities which had effected the commerce of neutral nations, and of the irritations and injuries produced by them, cannot but add to this confidence; and strengthens, at the same time, the hope, that wrongs committed on offending friends, under a pressure of circumstances, will now be reviewed with candor, and will be considered as founding just claims of retribution for the past and new assurances for the future.

Among our Indian neighbors, also, a spirit of peace and friendship generally prevails; and I am happy to inform you that the continued efforts to introduce among them the implements and the practice of husbandry, and of the household arts, have not been without success; that they are becoming more and more sensible of the superiority of this dependence for clothing and subsistence over the precarious resources of hunting and fishing; and already we are able to announce, that instead of that constant diminution of their numbers, produced by their wars and their wants, some of them begin to experience an increase of population.

To this state of general peace with which we have been blessed, one only exception exists. Tripoli, the least considerable of the Barbary States, had come forward with demands unfounded either in right or in compact,

---

Paul L. Ford, ed., *The Works of Thomas Jefferson,* Federal Edition, 12 vols. (New York: G. P. Putnam's Sons, 1904), 9:231–42.

ل had permitted itself to denounce war, on our failure to comply before a given day. The style of the demand admitted but one answer. I sent a small squadron of frigates into the Mediterranean, with assurances to that power of our sincere desire to remain in peace, but with orders to protect our commerce against the threatened attack. The measure was seasonable and salutary. The bey[4] had already declared war in form. His cruisers were out. Two had arrived at Gibraltar. Our commerce in the Mediterranean was blockaded, and that of the Atlantic in peril. The arrival of our squadron dispelled the danger. One of the Tripolitan cruisers having fallen in with, and engaged the small schooner *Enterprise,* commanded by Lieutenant Sterret, which had gone as a tender to our larger vessels, was captured, after a heavy slaughter of her men, without the loss of a single one on our part. The bravery exhibited by our citizens on that element, will, I trust, be a testimony to the world that it is not the want of that virtue which makes us seek their peace, but a conscientious desire to direct the energies of our nation to the multiplication of the human race, and not to its destruction. Unauthorized by the constitution, without the sanction of Congress, to go out beyond the line of defence, the vessel being disabled from committing further hostilities, was liberated with its crew. The legislature will doubtless consider whether, by authorizing measures of offence, also, they will place our force on an equal footing with that of its adversaries. I communicate all material information on this subject, that in the exercise of the important function considered by the constitution to the legislature exclusively, their judgment may form itself on a knowledge and consideration of every circumstance of weight. . . .

I lay before you the result of the census lately taken of our inhabitants, to a conformity with which we are to reduce the ensuing rates of representation and taxation. You will perceive that the increase of numbers during the last ten years, proceeding in geometrical ratio, promises a duplication in little more than twenty-two years. We contemplate this rapid growth, and the prospect it holds up to us, not with a view to the injuries it may enable us to do to others in some future day, but to the settlement of the extensive country still remaining vacant within our limits, to the multiplications of men susceptible of happiness, educated in the love of order, habituated to self-government, and value its blessings above all price.

Other circumstances, combined with the increase of numbers, have produced an augmentation of revenue arising from consumption, in a ratio far beyond that of population alone, and though the changes of foreign relations now taking place so desirably for the world, may for a season affect this branch of revenue, yet, weighing all probabilities of expense, as well as of income, there is reasonable ground of confidence that we may now safely dispense with all the internal taxes, comprehending ex-

[4]bey: ruler of Tripoli.

cises, stamps, auctions, licenses, carriages, and refined sugars, to which the postage on newspapers may be added, to facilitate the progress of information, and that the remaining sources of revenue will be sufficient to provide for the support of government to pay the interest on the public debts, and to discharge the principals in shorter periods than the laws or the general expectations had contemplated. War, indeed, and untoward events, may change this prospect of things, and call for expenses which the imposts could not meet; but sound principles will not justify our taxing the industry of our fellow citizens to accumulate treasure for wars to happen we know not when, and which might not perhaps happen but from the temptations offered by that treasure.

These views, however, of reducing our burdens, are formed on the expectation that a sensible, and at the same time a salutary reduction, may take place in our habitual expenditures. For this purpose, those of the civil government, the army, and navy, will need revisal.

When we consider that this government is charged with the external and mutual relations only of these states; that the states themselves have principal care of our persons, our property, and our reputation, constituting the great field of human concerns, we may well doubt whether our organization is not too complicated, too expensive; whether offices or officers have not been multiplied unnecessarily, and sometimes injuriously to the service they were meant to promote. I will cause to be laid before you an essay toward a statement of those who, under public employment of various kinds, draw money from the treasury or from our citizens. Time has not permitted a perfect enumeration, the ramifications of office being too multiplied and remote to be completely traced in a first trial. Among those who are dependent on executive discretion, I have begun the reduction of what was deemed necessary. The expenses of diplomatic agency have been considerably diminished. The inspectors of internal revenue who were found to obstruct the accountability of the institution, have been discontinued. . . .

An account of the receipts and expenditures of the last year, as prepared by the secretary of the treasury, will as usual be laid before you. The success which has attended the late sales of the public lands, shows that with attention they may be made an important source of receipt. Among the payments, those made in discharge of the principal and interest of the national debt, will show that the public faith has been exactly maintained. To these will be added an estimate of appropriations necessary for the ensuing year. This last will of course be effected by such modifications of the systems of expense, as you shall think proper to adopt.

A statement has been formed by the secretary of war, on mature consideration, of all the posts and stations where garrisons will be expedient, and of the number of men requisite for each garrison. The whole amount is considerably short of the present military establishment. For the surplus no particular use can be pointed out. For defence against invasion,

147

...per is as nothing; nor is it conceived needful or safe that a stand-
...should be kept up in time of peace for that purpose. Uncertain as
...ever be of the particular point in our circumference where an en-
...y choose to invade us, the only force which can be ready at every
point and competent to oppose them, is the body of neighboring citizens
as formed into a militia. On these, collected from the parts most convenient, in numbers proportioned to the invading foe, it is best to rely, not
only to meet the first attack, but if it threatens to be permanent, to maintain the defence until regulars may be engaged to relieve them. These
considerations render it important that we should at every session continue to amend the defects which from time to time show themselves in
the laws for regulating the militia, until they are sufficiently perfect. . . .

With respect to the extent to which our naval preparations should be
carried, some difference of opinion may be expected to appear; but just attention to the circumstances of every part of the Union will doubtless reconcile all. A small force will probably continue to be wanted for actual service in the Mediterranean. Whatever annual sum beyond that you may
think proper to appropriate to naval preparations, would perhaps be better
employed in providing those articles which may be kept without waste or
consumption, and be in readiness when any exigence calls them into use.
Progress has been made, as will appear by papers now communicated, in
providing materials for seventy-four gun ships as directed by law. . . .

Agriculture, manufactures, commerce, and navigation, the four pillars
of our prosperity, are the most thriving when left most free to individual
enterprise. Protection from casual embarrassments, however, may sometimes be seasonably interposed. If in the course of your observations or in-
quiries they should appear to need any aid within the limits of our constitutional powers, your sense of their importance is a sufficient assurance
they will occupy your attention. We cannot, indeed, but all feel an anxious
solicitude for the difficulties under which our carrying trade will soon be
placed. How far it can be relieved, otherwise than by time, is a subject of
important consideration. . . .

I cannot omit recommending a revisal of the laws on the subject of naturalization. Considering the ordinary chances of human life, a denial of cit-
izenship under a residence of fourteen years is a denial to a great proportion of those who ask it, and controls a policy pursued from their first
settlement by many of these States, and still believed of consequence to
their prosperity. And shall we refuse the unhappy fugitives from distress
that hospitality which the savages of the wilderness extended to our fathers arriving in this land? Shall oppressed humanity find no asylum on
this globe? The constitution, indeed, has wisely provided that, for admission to certain offices of important trust, a residence shall be required
sufficient to develop character and design. But might not the general character and capabilities of a citizen be safely communicated to every one

manifesting a *bona fide* purpose of embarking his life and fortunes permanently with us? with restrictions, perhaps, to guard against the fraudulent usurpation of our flag; an abuse which brings so much embarrassment and loss on the genuine citizen, and so much danger to the nation of being involved in war, that no endeavor should be spared to detect and suppress it.

These, fellow citizens, are the matters respecting the state of the nation, which I have thought of importance to be submitted to your consideration at this time. Some others of less moment, or not yet ready for communication, will be the subject of separate messages. I am happy in this opportunity of committing the arduous affairs of our government to the collected wisdom of the Union. Nothing shall be wanting on my part to inform, as far as in my power, the legislative judgment, nor to carry that judgment into faithful execution. The prudence and temperance of your discussions will promote, within your own walls, that conciliation which so much befriends national conclusion; and by its example will encourage among our constituents that progress of opinion which is tending to unite them in object and in will. That all should be satisfied with any one order of things is not to be expected, but I indulge the pleasing persuasion that the great body of our citizens will cordially concur in honest and disinterested efforts, which have for their object to preserve the general and State governments in their constitutional form and equilibrium; to maintain peace abroad, and order and obedience to the laws at home; to establish principles and practices of administration favorable to the security of liberty and prosperity, and to reduce expenses to what is necessary for the useful purposes of government.

On the day after Jefferson sent his first annual message to Congress, the full text was published in the Washington *National Intelligencer*. It soon appeared in newspapers throughout the nation and was also reprinted in Europe. Robert R. Livingston, the U.S. minister to France, wrote to Secretary of State James Madison from Paris on January 26, 1802, "The Presidents speech has been reprinted here and extremely admired. It sets our Country in the highest possible point of view — *but its contrast with what passes here is too striking to be relished by the people in power* who do *not like to speak* of it."[5]

[5]Livingston to Madison, Jan. 26, 1802, in J. C. A. Stagg et al., eds., *The Papers of James Madison: Secretary of State Series* (Charlottesville: University Press of Virginia, 1993), 2:423. Italics indicate words that have been decoded.

On December 12, 1801, Jefferson's message to Congress was reprinted in the *New-York Evening Post,* a Federalist paper recently founded with the support of Alexander Hamilton. Five days later, the newspaper published the first installment of a critique of the president's message. Signed "Lucius Crassus," the piece was written by Hamilton, who wrote seventeen additional installments before the series ended in April 1802.[6] A pamphlet edition, including all eighteen pieces, was also soon published.[7] In the first installment, or number, of the series, Hamilton directed his attention to the naval conflict with the Barbary pirates.

[6]Syrett et al., eds., *Hamilton Papers,* 25:449. Lucius Crassus was a noted orator and lawyer of ancient Rome and a strict follower of constitutional forms.
[7]*The Examination of the President's Message, at the Opening of Congress, December 7, 1801.* Revised and Corrected by the Author (New York: Printed and Published at the Office of the *New-York Evening Post,* 1802), ibid., pp. 449–50.

ALEXANDER HAMILTON

The Examination, Number I

December 17, 1801

[NEW YORK, DECEMBER 17, 1801]
Instead of delivering a *speech* to the House of Congress, at the opening of the present session, the President has thought fit to transmit a *Message.* Whether this has proceeded from pride or from humility, from a temperate love of reform, or from a wild spirit of innovation, is submitted to the conjectures of the curious. A single observation shall be indulged — since all agree, that he is unlike his predecessors in essential points, it is a mark of consistency to differ from them in matters of form.

Whoever considers the temper of the day, must be satisfied that this message is likely to add much to the popularity of our chief magistrate. It conforms, as far as would be tolerated at this early stage of our progress in political perfection, to the bewitching tenets of that illuminated doctrine, which promises man, ere long, an emancipation from the burdens and restraints of government; giving a foretaste of that pure felicity which the apostles of this doctrine have predicted. After having, with infinite

Harold C. Syrett et al., eds., *The Papers of Alexander Hamilton,* 27 vols. (New York: Columbia University Press, 1961–87), 25:453–57.

pains and assiduity, formed the public taste for this species of fare, it is certainly right for those whom the people have chosen for their caterers, to be attentive to the gratification of that taste. And should the viands, which they may offer, prove baneful poisons instead of wholesome aliments, the justification is both plain and easy—*Good patriots must, at all events, please the People.* But those whose patriotism is of the OLD SCHOOL, who differ so widely from the disciples of the new creed, that they would rather risk incurring the displeasure of the people, by speaking unpalatable truths, than betray their interest by fostering their prejudices; will never be deterred by an impure tide of popular opinion, from honestly pointing out the mistakes or the faults of weak or wicked men, who may have been selected as guardians of the public weal.

The Message of the President, by whatever motives it may have been dictated, is a performance which ought to alarm all who are anxious for the safety of our Government, for the respectability and welfare of our nation. It makes, or aims at making, a most prodigal sacrifice of constitutional energy, of sound principle, and of public interest, to the popularity of one man.

The first thing in it which excites our surprise, is the very extraordinary position, that though *Tripoli had declared war in form* against the United States, and had enforced it by actual hostility, yet that there was not power, for want of *the sanction of Congress,* to capture and detain her cruisers with their crews.

When the newspapers informed us, that one of these cruisers, after being subdued in a bloody conflict, had been liberated and permitted quietly to return home, the imagination was perplexed to divine the reason. The conjecture naturally was, that pursuing a policy, too refined perhaps for barbarians, it was intended by that measure to give the enemy a strong impression of our magnanimity and humanity. No one dreampt of a scruple as to the *right* to seize and detain the armed vessel of an open and avowed foe, vanquished in battle. The enigma is now solved, and we are presented with one of the most singular paradoxes, ever advanced by a man claiming the character of a statesman. When analyzed, it amounts to nothing less than this, that *between* two nations there may exist a state of complete war on the one side — of peace on the other.

War, of itself, gives to the parties a mutual right to kill in battle, and to capture the persons and property of each other. This is a rule of natural law; a necessary and inevitable consequence of the state of war. This state between two nations is completely produced by the act of one—it requires no concurrent act of the other. It is impossible to conceive the idea, that one nation can be in full war with another, and this other not in the same state with respect to its adversary. The moment therefore that two nations are, in an absolute sense, at war, the public force of each may exercise every act of hostility, which the general laws of war authorise, against the persons and property of the other. As it respects this conclusion, the distinction between offensive and defensive war, makes no difference. That distinction is only material to discriminate the aggressing nation from that which defends itself against attack. The war is offensive on the part of the state which makes it; on the opposite side it is defensive: but the rights of both, as to the measure of hostility, are equal.

It will be readily allowed that the Constitution of a particular country may limit the Organ charged with the direction of the public force, in the use or application of that force, even in time of actual war: but nothing short of the strongest negative words, of the most express prohibitions, can be admitted to restrain that Organ from so employing it, as to derive the fruits of actual victory, by making prisoners of the persons and detaining the property of a vanquished enemy. Our Constitution happily is not chargeable with so great an absurdity. The framers of it would have blushed at a provision, so repugnant to good sense, so inconsistent with national safety and inconvenience. That instrument has only provided affirmatively, that, "The Congress shall have power to declare War;" the plain meaning of which is that, it is the peculiar and exclusive province of Congress, *when the nation is at peace,* to change that state into a state of war; whether from calculations of policy or from provocations or injuries received: in other words, it belongs to Congress only, *to go to War.* But when a foreign nation declares, or openly and avowedly makes war upon the United States, they are then by the very fact, already *at war,* and any declaration on the part of Congress is nugatory: it is at least unnecessary. This inference is clear in principle, and has the sanction of established practice. It is clear in principle, because it is self-evident, that a declaration by one nation against another, produce[s] at once a complete state of war between both; and that no declaration on the other side can at all vary their relative situation: and in practice it is well known, that nothing is more common, than when war is declared by one party, to prosecute mutual hostilities, without a declaration by the other.

The doctrine of the Message includes the strange absurdity, that, without a declaration of war by Congress, our public force may destroy the life, but may not restrain the liberty, or seize the property of an enemy. This was exemplified in the very instance of the Tripolitan corsair.[8] A number of her crew were slaughtered in the combat, and after she was subdued she was set free with the remainder. But it may perhaps be said, that she was the assailant, and that resistance was an act of mere defence, and self-preservation. Let us then pursue the matter a step further. Our ships had blockaded the Tripolitan Admiral in the bay of Gibraltar; suppose, he had attempted to make his way out, without first firing upon them: if permitted

[8] corsair: privateer.

to do it, the blockade was a farce; if hindered by force, this would have amounted to more than a mere act of defence; and if a combat had ensued, we should then have seen an unequivocal illustration of the unintelligible right, to take the life but not to abridge the liberty, or capture the property of an enemy.

Let us suppose an invasion of our territory, previous to a declaration of war by Congress. The principle avowed in the Message would authorize our troops to kill those of the invader, if they should come within the reach of their bayonets, perhaps to drive them into the sea, and drown them; but not to disable them from doing harm, by the milder process of making them prisoners, and sending them into confinement. Perhaps it may be replied, that the same end would be answered by disarming and leaving them to starve. The merit of such an argument would be complete by adding, that should they not be famished, before the arrival of their ships, with a fresh supply of arms, we might then, if able, disarm them a second time, and send them on board their fleet, to return safely home.

The inconvenience of the doctrine in practice, is not less palpable than its folly in theory. In every case it presents a most unequal warfare. In the instance which has occurred, the vanquished Barbarian got off with the loss of his guns. Had he been victorious, the Americans, whose lives might have been spared, would have been doomed to wear out a miserable existence in slavery and chains. Substantial benefits would have rewarded his success; while on our side, life, liberty and property, were put in jeopardy, for an empty triumph. This, however, was a partial inconvenience — cases may arise in which evils of a more serious and comprehensive nature wou'd be the fruits of this visionary and fantastical principle. Suppose that, in the recess of Congress, a foreign maritime power should unexpectedly declare war against the United States, and send a fleet and army to seize Rhode-Island, in order from thence to annoy our trade and our seaport towns. Till the Congress should assemble and declare war, which would require time, our ships might, according to the hypothesis of the Message, be sent by the President to fight those of the enemy as often as they should be attacked, but not to capture and detain them: If beaten, both vessels and crews whould be lost to the United States: if successful, they could only disarm those they had overcome, and must suffer them to return to the place of common rendezvous, there to equip anew, for the purpose of resuming their depredations on our towns and our trade.

Who could restrain the laugh of derision at positions so preposterous, were it not for the reflection that in the first magistrate of our country, they cast a blemish on our national character? What will the world think of the fold when such is the shepherd?

LUCIUS CRASSUS.

try, there is an attempt to break down every pale which has been erected for the preservation of a national spirit and a national character; and to let in the most powerful means of perverting and corrupting both the one and the other.

This is more than the moderate opponents of Mr. Jefferson's elevation ever feared from his administration; much more than the most wrong-headed of his own sect dared to hope; it is infinitely more than any one who had read the fair professions in his Inaugural Speech could have suspected. Reflecting men must be dismayed at the prospect before us. If such rapid strides have been hazarded in the very gristle of his administration; what may be expected when it shall arrive to manhood? In vain was the collected wisdom of America convened at Philadelphia. In vain were the anxious labours of a Washington bestowed. Their works are regarded as nothing better than empty bubbles destined to be blown away from the mere breath of a disciple of *Turgot;*[10] a pupil of *Condorcet.*[11]

Though the most prominent features of the Message have been pourtrayed, and their deformity exhibited in true colors; there remain many less important traits not yet touched, which, however, will materially assist us in determining its true character. To particularise them with minuteness would employ more time and labor than the object deserves; yet to pass them by wholly, without remark, would be to forego valuable materials for illustrating the true nature of the performance under examination.

There remains to be cursorily noticed, a disposition in our Chief Magistrate, far more partial to the state governments, than to our national government; to pull down rather than to build up our Federal edifice — to vilify the past administration of the latter — to court for himself popular favor by artifices not to be approved of, either for their dignity, their candor or their patriotism.

Why are we emphatically and fastidiously told, that "the States individually have the *principal* care of our *persons* our *property* and our *reputation, constituting the great field of human concerns."* Was it to render the State Governments more dear to us, more the objects of affectionate solicitude? Nothing surely was necessary on this head; they are already the favourites of the people, and if they do not forfeit the advantage by a most gross abuse of trust, must, by the very nature of the objects confided to them, continue always to be so. Was it then to prevent too large a portion of affection from being bestowed on the general Government. No pains on this

---

[10]Anne Robert Jacques Turgot, Baron de l'Aulne, was a French economist. Both Turgot and Jefferson — in varying degrees — were Physiocrats who believed in various reforms for the improvement of mankind.

[11]Marie Jean Antoine Nicholas Caritat, Marquis de Condorcet, was a French mathematician and philosopher who supported the French Revolution in its early stages, but he died in jail in 1794. As U.S. minister to France, Jefferson became a close friend of Condorcet.

head were requisite, not only for the reason just assigned, but for the further reason that the more peculiar objects of this Government, though no less essential to our prosperity than those of the State Governments, oblige it often to act upon the community in a manner more likely to produce aversion than fondness. Accordingly every day furnishes proof, that it is not the *spoiled child of the many.* On this point the high example of the President himself is pregnant with instruction. Was it to indicate the supreme importance of the State Governments over that of the United States? This was as little useful, as it was correct. Considering the vast variety of humours, prepossessions and localities, which in the much diversified composition of these states, militate against the weight and authority of the general Government, if union under that government is necessary, it can answer no valuable purpose to depreciate its importance in the eyes of the people. It is not correct; because to the care of the Federal Government are confided directly, those great general interests on which all particular interests materially depend: our safety in respect to foreign nations; our tranquility in respect to each other; the foreign and mutual commerce of the states; the establishment and regulation of the money of the country; the management of our national finances; indirectly, the security of liberty by the guarantee of a republican form of government to each state; the security of property by the interdiction of laws violating the obligation of contracts & issuing the emissions of paper money under state authority; (from both of which causes the right of property had experienced serious injury); the prosperity of agriculture and manufactures as intimately connected with that of commerce, and as depending in a variety of ways upon the agency of the general Government: In a word, it is the province of the general Government to manage the greatest number of those concerns in which its provident *activity* and *exertion* are of most importance to the people; and we have only to compare the state of our country antecedent to its establishment, with what it has been since, to be convinced that the most operative causes of public prosperity depend upon that general Government. It is not meant, by what has been said, to insinuate that the state Governments are not extremely useful in their proper spheres; but the object is to guard against the mischiefs of exaggerating their importance in derogation from that of the general Government. Every attempt to do this is, remotely, a stab at the Union of these states; a blow to our collective existence as one people — and to all the blessings which are interwoven with that sacred fraternity.

If it be true as insinuated that "our organization is too complicated — too expensive"— let it be simplified; let this, however, be done in such a manner as not to mutilate, weaken and eventually destroy our present system, but in a manner to increase the energy, and insure the duration of our national Government THE ROCK OF OUR POLITICAL SALVATION.

In this insinuation, and in the suggestion that "offices and officers have been unnecessarily multiplied:" in the intimation that appropriations have not been sufficiently specific, and that the system of accountability to a single department has been disturbed; in this and in other things, too minute to be particularized, we discover new proofs of the disposition of the present Executive, unjustly and indecorously to arraign his predecessors.

As far as the Message undertakes to specify any instance of the improper complexity of our organization, namely, in the instance of the Judiciary Establishment, the late administration has been already vindicated.

As to the "*undue* multiplication of offices and officers," it is substantially a misrepresentation. It would be nothing less than a miracle, if in a small number of instances, it had not happened that particular offices and officers might have been dispensed with. For in the early essays of a new government, in making the various establishments relative to the affairs of a nation, some mistakes in this respect will arise, notwithstanding the greatest caution. It must happen to every government that in the hurry of a new plan, some agents will occasionally be employed who may not be absolutely necessary; and this, where there is every inclination to œconomy. Similar things may have happened under our past administration. But any competent judge, who will take the trouble to examine into it, will be convinced, that there is no just cause for blame in this particular.

The President has not pointed out the causes to which he applies the charge; but he has communicated information of some retrenchments which he has made, and probably intends that the truth shall be inferred from this. . . .

By the time Hamilton finished *The Examination* and his concluding number was published in the *New-York Evening Post* on April 8, 1802, Congress was well on its way to finishing its business for the session. Adjournment came on May 3. That was none too soon for Hamilton, who early in June wrote to his Federalist friend Rufus King, the U.S. minister to Great Britain, "You have seen the course of the Administration hitherto, especially during the last session of Congress; and I am persuaded you will agree in opinion with me that it could hardly have been more diligent in mischief." [12]

The Examination not having attracted much attention, Hamilton did not undertake to review Jefferson's second annual message to Congress of December 15, 1802. In late December, he wrote to fellow Federalist Charles Cotesworth Pinckney, "In my opinion the follies and vices of the

---

[12] Hamilton to King, June 3, 1802, in Syrett et al., eds., *Hamilton Papers,* 26:12.

Administration have as yet made no material impression to their disadvantage. On the contrary, I think the malady is rather progressive than upon the decline in our Northern Quarter." Referring to Jefferson's most recent message, he continued, "The last *lullaby* message, instead of inspiring contempt, attracts praise. Mankind are forever destined to be the dupes of bold and cunning imposture."[13]

Soon after Hamilton had finished his commentaries on Jefferson's first annual message, other national concerns diverted attention from Hamilton's repetitious essays. In April 1802, Jefferson wrote, "Every eye in the U.S. is now fixed on this affair of Louisiana. Perhaps nothing since the revolutionary war has produced more uneasy sensations through the body of the nation."[14] The crisis to which Jefferson referred had been building since Spain secretly retroceded Louisiana to France soon after Jefferson took office as president. In a long letter to Robert R. Livingston, the U.S. minister to France, Jefferson expanded on the Louisiana situation.

[13] Hamilton to Pinckney, Dec. 29, 1802, ibid., p. 71.
[14] Jefferson to Robert R. Livingston, April 18, 1802, in Ford, ed., *Jefferson Works,* 9:368.

THOMAS JEFFERSON

Letter to Robert R. Livingston

April 18, 1802

. . . The cession of Louisiana and the Floridas by Spain to France works most sorely on the U. S. On this subject the Secretary of State has written to you fully. Yet I cannot forbear recurring to it personally, so deep is the impression it makes in my mind. It compleatly reverses all the political relations of the U. S. and will form a new epoch in our political course. Of all nations of any consideration France is the one which hitherto has offered the fewest points on which we could have any conflict of right, and the most points of a communion of interests. From these causes we have ever looked to her as our *natural friend,* as one with which we never could have an occasion of difference. Her growth therefore we viewed as our own, her misfortunes ours. There is on the globe one single spot, the possessor of

Paul L. Ford, ed., *The Works of Thomas Jefferson,* Federal Edition, 12 vols. (New York: G. P. Putnam's Sons, 1904), 9:364–68.

which is our natural and habitual enemy. It is New Orleans, through which the produce of three-eighths of our territory must pass to market, and from its fertility it will ere long yield more than half of our whole produce and contain more than half our inhabitants. France placing herself in that door assumes to us the attitude of defiance. Spain might have retained it quietly for years. Her pacific dispositions, her feeble state, would induce her to increase our facilities there, so that her possession of the place would be hardly felt by us, and it would not perhaps be very long before some circumstance might arise which might make the cession of it to us the price of something of more worth to her. Not so can it ever be in the hands of France. The impetuosity of her temper, the energy and restlessness of her character, placed in a point of eternal friction with us, and our character, which though quiet, and loving peace and the pursuit of wealth, is high-minded, despising wealth in competition with insult or injury, enterprising and energetic as any nation on earth, these circumstances render it impossible that France and the U. S. can continue long friends when they meet in so irritable a position. They as well as we must be blind if they do not see this; and we must be very improvident if we do not begin to make arrangements on that hypothesis. The day that France takes possession of N. Orleans fixes the sentence which is to restrain her forever within her low water mark. It seals the union of two nations who in conjunction can maintain exclusive possession of the ocean. From that moment we must marry ourselves to the British fleet and nation. We must turn all our attentions to a maritime force, for which our resources place us on very high grounds: and having formed and cemented together a power which may render reinforcement of her settlements here impossible to France, make the first cannon, which shall be fired in Europe the signal for tearing up any settlement she may have made, and for holding the two continents of America in sequestration for the common purposes of the united British and American nations. This is not a state of things we seek or desire. It is one which this measure, if adopted by France, forces on us, as necessarily as any other cause, by the laws of nature, brings on its necessary effect. It is not from a fear of France that we deprecate this measure proposed by her. For however greater her force is than ours compared in the abstract, it is nothing in comparison of ours when to be exerted on our soil. But it is from a sincere love of peace, and a firm persuasion that bound to France by the interests and the strong sympathies still existing in the minds of our citizens, and holding relative positions which insure their continuance we are secure of a long course of peace. Whereas the change of friends, which will be rendered necessary if France changes that position, embarks us necessarily as a belligerent power in the first war of Europe. In that case France will have held possession of New Orleans during the interval of a peace, long or short, at the end of which it will be wrested from her. Will this short-lived possession have been an equivalent to her for the transfer of such a weight into the scale of her enemy? Will not the amalgamation of a young, thriving, nation continue to that enemy the health and force which are at present so evidently on the decline? And will a few years possession of N. Orleans add equally to the strength of France? She may say she needs Louisiana for the supply of her West Indies. She does not need it in time of peace. And in war she could not depend on them because they would be so easily intercepted. I should suppose that all these considerations might in some proper form be brought into view of the government of France. Tho' stated by us, it ought not to give offence; because we do not bring them forward as a menace, but as consequences not controulable by us, but inevitable from the course of things. We mention them not as things which we desire by any means, but as things we deprecate; and we beseech a friend to look forward and to prevent them for our common interests.

If France considers Louisiana however as indispensable for her views she might perhaps be willing to look about for arrangements which might reconcile it to our interests. If anything could do this it would be the ceding to us the island of New Orleans and the Floridas. This would certainly in a great degree remove the causes of jarring and irritation between us, and perhaps for such a length of time as might produce other means of making the measure permanently conciliatory to our interests and friendships. It would at any rate relieve us from the necessity of taking immediate measures for countervailing such an operation by arrangements in another quarter. Still we should consider N. Orleans and the Floridas as equivalent for the risk of a quarrel with France. . . . Every eye in the U. S. is now fixed on this affair of Louisiana. Perhaps nothing since the revolutionary war has produced more uneasy sensations through the body of the nation. Notwithstanding temporary bickerings have taken place with France, she has still a strong hold on the affections of our citizens generally. I have thought it not amiss, by way of supplement to the letters of the Secretary of State to write you this private one to impress you with the importance we affix to this transaction. . . .

By November 1802, the situation had become even more explosive, when the intendant[15] at New Orleans suspended the right of Americans to deposit goods there awaiting shipment abroad. Although Jefferson and Secretary of State Madison moved promptly to deal with the critical situation, Jefferson did not report their progress in his annual message to Congress in December 1802 — the message that Hamilton called a "lullaby."[16]

[15]intendant: administrative official or governor.
[16]Hamilton to Pinckney, Dec. 29, 1802, in Syrett et al., eds., *Hamilton Papers,* 26:71.

On January 11, 1803, President Jefferson sent to the Senate the nomination of James Monroe as a special emissary to France and Spain to negotiate on the Louisiana crisis. Over Federalist opposition, the nomination was speedily confirmed. Joining in the Federalist dissent to the appointment of Monroe, Hamilton prepared for the press the following article, signed "Pericles," explaining the policy he thought the president should adopt.

ALEXANDER HAMILTON

New-York Evening Post

February 8, 1803

[NEW YORK, FEBRUARY 8, 1803]
Since the question of Independence, none has occurred more deeply interesting to the United States than the cession of Louisiana to France. This event threatens the early dismemberment of a large portion of our country: more immediately the safety of all the Southern States; and remotely the independence of the whole union. This is the portentous aspect which the affair presents to all men of sound and reflecting minds of whatever party, and it is not to be concealed that the only question which now offers itself, is, how is the evil to be averted?

The strict right to resort at once to WAR, if it should be deemed expedient cannot be doubted. *A manifest and great danger* to the nation: the nature of the cession to France, extending to ancient limits without respect to our rights by treaty; the direct infraction of an important article of the treaty itself in withholding the deposition of New-Orleans; either of these affords justifiable cause of WAR and that they would authorize immediately hostilities, is not to be questioned by the most scrupulous mind.

The whole is then a question of expediency. Two courses only present. First, to negociate and endeavour to purchase, and if this fails to go to war. Secondly, to seize at once on the Floridas and New-Orleans, and then negociate.

A strong objection offers itself to the first. There is not the most remote probability that the ambitious and aggrandizing views of [Napoleon] Bonaparte will commute the territory for money. Its acquisition is of immense importance to France, and has long been an object of her extreme

Harold C. Syrett et al., eds., *The Papers of Alexander Hamilton,* 27 vols. (New York: Columbia University Press, 1961–87), 26:82–85.

solicitude. The attempt therefore to purchase, in the first instance, will certainly fail, and in the end, war must be resorted to, under all the accumulation of difficulties caused by a previous and strongly fortified possession of the country by our adversary.

The second plan is, therefore, evidently the best. First, because effectual: the acquisition easy; the preservation afterwards easy: The evils of a war with France at this time are certainly not very formidable: Her fleet crippled and powerless, her treasury empty, her resources almost dried up, in short, gasping for breath after a tremendous conflict which, though it left her victorious, left her nearly exhausted under her extraordinary exertions. On the other hand, we might count with certainty on the aid of Great Britain with her powerful navy.

Secondly, this plan is preferable because it affords us the only chance of avoiding a long-continued war. When we have once taken possession, the business will present itself to France in a new aspect. She will then have to weigh the immense difficulties, if not the utter impracticability of wresting it from us. In this posture of affairs she will naturally conclude it is her interest to bargain. Now it may become expedient to terminate hostilities by a purchase, and a cheaper one may reasonably be expected.

To secure the better prospect of final success, the following auxiliary measures ought to be adopted.

The army should be increased to ten thousand men, for the purpose of insuring the preservation of the conquest. Preparations for increasing our naval force should be made. The militia should be classed, and effectual provision made for raising on an emergency, 40,000 men. Negociations should be pushed with Great-Britain, to induce her to hold herself in readiness to co-operate fully with us, at a moment's warning.

This plan should be adopted and proclaimed before the departure of our envoy.

Such measures would astonish and disconcert Bonaparte himself; our envoy would be enabled to speak and treat with effect; and all Europe would be taught to respect us.

These ideas have been long entertained by the writer, but he has never given himself the trouble to commit them to the public, because he despaired of their being adopted. They are now thrown out with very little hope of their producing any change in the conduct of administration, yet, with the encouragement that there is a strong current of public feeling in favour of decisive measures.

If the President would adopt this course, he might yet retrieve his character; induce the best part of the community to look favorably on his political career, exalt himself in the eyes of Europe, save the country, and secure a permanent fame. But for this, alas! Jefferson is not destined!

PERICLES.

A month after Hamilton wrote the preceding piece, James Monroe departed from New York for Paris carrying instructions and authority to offer up to fifty million livres — slightly more than $9 million — for New Orleans and the Floridas.[17] On April 30, 1803, Monroe and Robert R. Livingston, the U.S. minister to France, initialed the agreement that ceded all of Louisiana to the United States for $15 million. Having failed to suppress a revolution in Santo Domingo and reclaim that island colony, Napoleon regarded Louisiana as vulnerable to conquest. The treaty was formally signed on May 2, but the report of the signing did not reach New York until June 30. It was July 3 before the news reached Washington, D.C. Meanwhile, Hamilton had been drafting a piece for publication, which appeared on July 5.

[17] Madison to Robert R. Livingston and James Monroe, Mar. 2, 1803, in Gaillard Hunt, ed., *The Writings of James Madison,* 9 vols. (New York: G. P. Putnam's Sons, 1900–1910), 7:19, 24–25.

ALEXANDER HAMILTON

New-York Evening Post

July 5, 1803

[NEW YORK, JULY 5, 1803]
Purchase of Louisiana. At length the business of New-Orleans has terminated favourably to this country. Instead of being obliged to rely any longer on the force of treaties, for a place of deposit, the jurisdiction of the territory is now transferred to our hands and in future the navigation of the Mississippi will be ours unmolested. This, it will be allowed is an important acquisition, not, indeed, as territory, but as being essential to the peace and prosperity of our Western country, and as opening a free and valuable market to our commercial states. This purchase has been made during the period of Mr. Jefferson's presidency, and, will, doubtless, give eclat to his administration. Every man, however, possessed of the least candour and reflection will readily acknowledge that the acquisition has been solely owing to a fortuitous concurrence of unforseen and unexpected circumstances, and not to any wise or vigorous measures on the part of the American government.

Harold C. Syrett et al., eds., *The Papers of Alexander Hamilton,* 27 vols. (New York: Columbia University Press, 1961–87), 26:129–31.

As soon as we experienced from Spain a direct infraction of an important article of our treaty, in withholding the deposit of New-Orleans, it afforded us justifiable cause of war, and authorised immediate hostilities. Sound policy unquestionably demanded of us to begin with a prompt, bold and vigorous resistance against the injustice: to seize the object at once; and having this *vantage ground,* should we have thought it advisable to terminate hostilities by a purchase, we might then have done it on almost our own terms. This course, however, was not adopted, and we were about to experience the fruits of our folly, when another nation has found it her interest to place the French Government in a situation substantially as favourable to our views and interests as those recommended by the federal party here, excepting indeed that we should probably have obtained the same object on better terms.

On the part of France the short interval of peace had been wasted in repeated and fruitless efforts to subjugate St. Domingo; and those means which were originally destined to the colonization of Louisiana, had been gradually exhausted by the unexpected difficulties of this ill-starred enterprize.

To the deadly climate of St. Domingo, and to the courage and obstinate resistance made by its black inhabitants are we indebted for the obstacles which delayed the colonization of Louisiana, till the auspicious moment, when a rupture between England and France gave a new turn to the projects of the latter, and destroyed at once all her schemes as to this favourite object of her ambition.

It was made known to Bonaparte, that among the first objects of England would be the seizure of New-Orleans, and that preparations were even then in a state of forwardness for that purpose. The First Consul[18] could not doubt, that if an English fleet was sent thither, the place must fall without resistance; it was obvious, therefore, that it would be in every shape preferable that it should be placed in the possession of a neutral power; and when, besides, some millions of money, of which he was extremely in want, were offered him, to part with what he could no longer hold it affords a moral certainty, that it was to an accidental state of circumstances, and not to wise plans, that this cession, at this time, has been owing. We shall venture to add, that neither of the ministers through whose instrumentality it was effected, will ever deny this, or even pretend that previous to the time when a rupture was believed to be inevitable, there was the smallest chance of inducing the First Consul, with his ambitious and aggrandizing views, to commute the territory for any sum of money in their power to offer. The real truth is, Bonaparte found himself absolutely compelled by situation, to relinquish his darling plan of colonising the banks of the Mississippi: and thus have the Government of the United States, by the unforseen operation of events, gained what the fee-

[18] First Consul: Bonaparte.

bleness and pusillanimity of its miserable system of measures could never have acquired. Let us then, with all due humility, acknowledge this as another of those signal instances of the kind interpositions of an over-ruling Providence, which we more especially experienced during our revolutionary war, & by which we have more than once, been saved from the consequences of our errors and perverseness. . . .

The purchase of Louisiana marked the zenith of Jefferson's first term as president. By 1804, as Jefferson's reelection seemed increasingly certain, some Federalist leaders in New England talked among themselves about seceding from the United States and forming a northern confederacy. They considered plans to hold a meeting in Boston in the fall of 1804 and reportedly expected Hamilton to attend. Years later, John Quincy Adams recalled that in April 1804, Rufus King told him that former Secretary of State Timothy Pickering had talked about such a northern confederacy with Hamilton. King also said that Hamilton had disapproved entirely of such a movement.[19] Writing to Federalist Theodore Sedgwick, a former Speaker of the House of Representatives, Hamilton reaffirmed his opposition to any dismemberment of the union.

[19] Syrett et al., eds., *Hamilton Papers,* 26:310; Henry Adams, ed., *Documents Relating to New-England Federalism, 1800–1815* (Boston: Little, Brown, 1905), pp. 147–48.

ALEXANDER HAMILTON

Letter to Theodore Sedgwick

July 10, 1804

NEW YORK JULY 10. 1804.

My Dear Sir:
I have received two letters from you since we last saw each other — that of the latest date being the 24 of May. I have had in mind for some time a long letter to you, explaining my view of the course and tendency of our

Harold C. Syrett et al., eds., *The Papers of Alexander Hamilton,* 27 vols. (New York: Columbia University Press, 1961–87), 26:309–10.

Politics, and my intentions as to my own future conduct. But my plan embraced so large a range that owing to much avocation, some indifferent health, and a growing distaste for Politics, the letter is still considerably short of being finished. I write this now to satisfy you, that want of regard for you has not been the cause of my silence.

I will here express but one sentiment, which is, that Dismemberment of our Empire will be a clear sacrifice of great positive advantages, without any counterballancing good; administering no relief to our real Disease; which is DEMOCRACY, the poison of which by a subdivision will only be the more concerned in each part, and consequently the more virulent.

King is on his way for Boston where you may chance to see him, and hear from himself his sentiments.

God bless you   A H

T Sedgwick Esqr

Tragically, this letter was among the last letters that Alexander Hamilton would ever write. Tensions between Hamilton and Vice President Aaron Burr had mounted following Burr's defeat for election as governor of New York in April 1804. Hamilton, who had played a major role in Burr's defeat, was reported to have made derogatory remarks about Burr, and when Burr demanded an explanation, a duel resulted.

In the early morning hours of July 11, 1804, Hamilton, accompanied by his second and a physician, crossed the Hudson River to the New Jersey shore, where Aaron Burr was already waiting. In the duel that followed, Hamilton was mortally wounded by the first shot from Burr's pistol. He died a painful death the following afternoon.[20]

Jefferson's voluminous extant papers are virtually silent on the death of Hamilton. Although Burr had been estranged from Jefferson since the election of 1800, he was still vice president of the United States in 1804. Noting the absence of commentary on Hamilton's death in Jefferson's letters, Jefferson biographer Dumas Malone observed that "no contrast could be greater than that between this extraordinarily dramatic and

---

[20] Documents and letters relating to the duel between Hamilton and Burr fill 114 pages in Syrett et al., eds., *Hamilton Papers,* 26:235–349. See also editorial note and documents in Mary-Jo Kline and Joanne Wood Ryan, eds., *Political Correspondence and Public Papers of Aaron Burr,* 2 vols. (Princeton: Princeton University Press, 1983), 2:876–89.

deeply tragic episode and the virtual silence with which [Jefferson] greeted it."[21]

Thomas Jefferson would live another twenty-two years following the death of Alexander Hamilton. Reelected as president in 1804, Jefferson would find his second term to be less successful than his first. The continuing Napoleonic wars in Europe challenged America's neutrality, and Jefferson's embargo policy failed to achieve its aim of influencing events in Europe. When March 1809 arrived, Jefferson was ready to retire to Monticello.

Jefferson's retirement years were busy ones, filled with continuing construction at Monticello, the pursuit of scientific farming, and the founding of the University of Virginia. In that final accomplishment, Jefferson was the key figure in gaining legislative support, and he became the architect of the first buildings and the planner of the curriculum. In one of his last public appearances, Jefferson hosted a dinner for Lafayette in the recently completed dome room of the Rotunda of the University of Virginia in November 1824. The university opened on March 7, 1825, and Jefferson wrote soon after that he was "closing the last scenes of life by fashioning and fostering an establishment for the instruction of those who are to come after us."[22]

In one of the extraordinary occurrences of the early republic, Jefferson died at Monticello on July 4, 1826, the fiftieth anniversary of the Declaration of Independence. On the same day, John Adams died in Quincy, Massachusetts. By the time of their deaths, Hamilton would be remembered, not because of his tragic death, but because of his role and influence in setting the direction of the young republic.

[21] Dumas Malone, *Jefferson the President, First Term, 1801–1805* (Boston: Little, Brown, 1970), p. 425.
[22] Jefferson to Augustus B. Woodward, Apr. 3, 1825, in Ford, ed., *Jefferson Works,* 12:408.

Epilogue: The Legacies of Jefferson and Hamilton

Despite the vast differences between Thomas Jefferson and Alexander Hamilton, both men contributed greatly to the shaping of the American nation in its formative years. Jefferson, the older of the two men, as the principal drafter of the Declaration of Independence and the wartime governor of Virginia, risked his life in the American Revolution. As a soldier on the battlefield, Hamilton too risked his life during the Revolution. During that war, Hamilton gained the respect and favor of General George Washington, an association that would greatly shape his postwar career. As a member of the Constitutional Convention of 1787 in Philadelphia, Hamilton had an active role in the making and adoption of the Constitution of the United States. At that time Jefferson was actively engaged in Paris as the U.S. minister to France.

Jefferson and Hamilton had their first major contacts and their longest period of working in close association while Hamilton was the secretary of the Treasury and Jefferson was the secretary of state in President Washington's first cabinet. Here their differences were frequently

---

Figure 10. (opposite) *Engraving of Alexander Hamilton, by William Rollinson.* Published at the Columbia Academy of Painting in New York in 1804, less than two months after Hamilton's death, the print offered an image taken from a portrait by Archibald Robertson. Hamilton is pictured standing beside a table with books, papers, inkstand, and quill. One packet is labeled "Liberty of the Press." Another paper is marked "Carriage Tax." On shelves above, Hamilton's military hat and sword are pictured with the medal of the Society of the Cincinnati hanging from the sword hilt. A bundle of papers marked "Report on Funding the Public Debt" is tied with a ribbon and the seal of the Department of the Treasury. National Portrait Gallery, Smithsonian Institution.

intense, and Hamilton was the most influential adviser in shaping the president's positions. Washington based his domestic policy largely on Hamilton's economic initiatives in the funding of the national debt, the assumption of state debts, an excise tax, and the chartering of a national bank. Meanwhile, as secretary of state, Jefferson gave firm direction to American foreign policies, although at times not without interference from Hamilton. Despite their differences, both men played immensely important roles in directing the course of the young republic under the new Constitution.

Jefferson's election as president in the contest of 1800 — which Hamilton's opposition in the political struggle in New York had failed to defeat — brought Jefferson to a height of political power and national respect that Hamilton would never achieve. Hamilton's final years, before his death in the duel with Aaron Burr in 1804, were politically frustrating. Had he lived as long as Jefferson, however, he would have seen much of the program that he had initiated as secretary of the Treasury become accepted national policy. Especially notable was the decision of the Supreme Court under Chief Justice John Marshall in *McCulloch v. Maryland* (1819) declaring a national bank to be constitutional — a decision that gave judicial sanction to the doctrine of implied powers subscribed to by Hamilton as a member of Washington's cabinet.

In the years after Hamilton's death, Jefferson only rarely made reference to him in his correspondence. Jefferson never endorsed a national bank, nor did he approve of Marshall's opinion on its constitutionality. At the same time, Jefferson moved toward Hamilton's views in regard to tariffs and manufacturing. The change began during Jefferson's presidency with the embargo of 1807, and the War of 1812 convinced him of the necessity of developing domestic manufactures. Jefferson approved of the tariff of 1816, giving support to infant manufacturing industries.

As the author of the Declaration of Independence and the third president of the United States, Thomas Jefferson today enjoys a more commanding presence in the nation's memory than Alexander Hamilton does. The imposing Jefferson Memorial occupies a strikingly large place in the nation's capital. Less widely noticed is the statue of Hamilton that stands outside the Treasury Department building in Washington.

At the same time, in the daily circulation of Federal Reserve notes, Hamilton today enjoys a more commanding presence than Jefferson. Whereas Jefferson's portrait appears on the rarely used $2 bill, Hamilton's portrait on the $10 bill is a daily reminder to millions of people of the man who played a major role in setting the course for the financial stability and economic growth of the young American republic.

Thomas Jefferson lies buried on his beloved hilltop at Monticello, sheltered from the bustle of cities that he so much disliked. Alexander Hamilton fittingly lies buried in the Trinity Churchyard near the hustle and action of Wall Street in New York City. After two hundred years, the influences of both men still persist and compete.

A Jefferson and Hamilton Chronology
(1743–1826)

1743   *April 13:* Thomas Jefferson is born at Shadwell in Goochland (now Albemarle) County, Virginia.

1755   *[January 11]:* Alexander Hamilton is born on the British-held island of Nevis in the West Indies.

1757   Jefferson's father dies.

1758–
1760   Jefferson attends the Latin school conducted by the Reverend James Maury.

1760–
1762   Jefferson attends the College of William and Mary in Williamsburg, Virginia.

1762   Jefferson begins to study law under George Wythe in Williamsburg.

1768   After the death of his mother, Hamilton becomes an apprentice clerk in a mercantile firm on Saint Croix.

1772   *January 1:* Jefferson marries Martha Wayles Skelton.

1773   Hamilton arrives in New York from the West Indies.

1774   Jefferson writes *A Summary View of the Rights of British America.*
Hamilton writes *A Full Vindication of the Measures of Congress.*

1775   Jefferson attends the Continental Congress in Philadelphia.
Hamilton is appointed captain of artillery by the New York Provincial Congress.

1776   Jefferson drafts the Declaration of Independence.
Hamilton engages in military action in New York and New Jersey.

1777   Hamilton is appointed as an aide to General Washington, with the rank of lieutenant colonel.

1779   Jefferson is elected governor of Virginia.

1780   Jefferson is reelected governor.
Hamilton marries Elizabeth Schuyler in New York.

1781   Hamilton resigns from General Washington's staff.
Hamilton sees combat in the battle of Yorktown.

1782   Hamilton serves as a New York delegate to the Continental Congress.
Jefferson's wife dies.

1783   Jefferson serves as a Virginia delegate to the Continental Congress.
Hamilton opens a law office in New York.

1785   Jefferson is appointed U.S. minister to France.

1787   Hamilton serves as a New York delegate to the federal Constitutional Convention in Philadelphia in May. Returns to the United States in November.
Hamilton's first *Federalist* paper is published.
Jefferson publishes his *Notes on the State of Virginia.*

1789   Jefferson attends the opening meeting of the French Estates General at Versailles.
Hamilton is appointed secretary of the Treasury in Washington's administration.

1790   Jefferson accepts appointment as secretary of state in Washington's administration.
Hamilton presents his *Report on a National Bank.*

1791   Jefferson argues that a national bank is unconstitutional.
Hamilton defends a national bank as constitutional.
Hamilton presents his *Report on Manufactures.*

1793   Jefferson resigns as secretary of state at the end of the year.

1794   Hamilton takes the field to lead the army to suppress the Whiskey Rebellion in Pennsylvania.

1795   Hamilton resigns as secretary of the Treasury.

1797   Jefferson is installed as president of the American Philosophical Society in Philadelphia.
Jefferson is inaugurated as vice president of the United States.

1798   Hamilton is appointed Inspector General of the Army, with the rank of major general.

1800   Hamilton retires from the army.

1801   Jefferson is elected as the third president of the United States and is inaugurated on March 4.
Hamilton writes the first of a series of articles critical of President Jefferson's policies.

1803   The United States purchases Louisiana.

1804   *July 11:* Alexander Hamilton is mortally wounded in a duel with Aaron Burr and dies the following day.
Jefferson is reelected president of the United States.

1805   *March 4:* Jefferson is inaugurated as president for a second term.

1809   Jefferson retires from the presidency and returns to Monticello.

1817   Jefferson lays the cornerstone of the first building to become part of the University of Virginia.

1825   *March:* As the founder, Jefferson witnesses the opening of the University of Virginia to students.

1826   *July 4:* Thomas Jefferson dies at Monticello on the fiftieth anniversary of the Declaration of Independence.

Selected Bibliography

Adams, Charles Francis, ed. *The Memoirs of John Quincy Adams, Comprising Portions of His Diary from 1797 to 1848.* 12 vols. Philadelphia: J. B. Lippincott, 1874–77.

Appleby, Joyce. *Capitalism and a New Social Order: The Republican Vision of the 1790s.* New York: New York University Press, 1984.

Banning, Lance. *The Jefferson Persuasion: The Evolution of Party Ideology.* Ithaca: Cornell University Press, 1978.

Bowling, Kenneth R., and Helen E. Veit, eds. *The Diary of William Maclay and Other Notes on Senate Debates.* Vol. 9 of *Documentary History of the First Federal Congress of the United States of America, March 4, 1789– March 3, 1791.* Baltimore: Johns Hopkins University Press, 1978.

Boyd, Julian P. *Number 7: Alexander Hamilton's Secret Attempts to Control American Foreign Policy.* Princeton: Princeton University Press, 1964.

Boyd, Julian P., Charles T. Cullen, and John Catanzariti, eds. *The Papers of Thomas Jefferson.* 27 vols. to date. Princeton: Princeton University Press, 1950–.

Combs, Jerald A. *The Jay Treaty: Political Battleground of the Founding Fathers.* Berkeley: University of California Press, 1970.

Cooke, Jacob Ernest. *Alexander Hamilton.* New York: Charles Scribner's Sons, 1982.

Cunningham, Noble E., Jr. *In Pursuit of Reason: The Life of Thomas Jefferson.* Baton Rouge: Louisiana State University Press, 1987.

Cunningham, Noble E., Jr. *The Jeffersonian Republicans: The Formation of Party Organization, 1789–1801.* Chapel Hill: University of North Carolina Press, 1957.

Cunningham, Noble E., Jr. *The Process of Government under Jefferson.* Princeton: Princeton University Press, 1978.

DePauw, Linda Grant, Charlene Bangs Bickford, and Helen E. Veit, eds. *Documentary History of the First Federal Congress of the United States of America.* 14 vols. Baltimore: Johns Hopkins University Press, 1972–98.

Elkins, Stanley, and Eric McKitrick. *The Age of Federalism: The American Republic, 1788–1800.* New York: Oxford University Press, 1993.

Flaumenhaft, Harvey. *The Effective Republic: Administration and Constitution in the Thought of Alexander Hamilton.* Durham: Duke University Press, 1992.

Flexner, James Thomas. *The Young Hamilton: A Biography.* Boston: Little, Brown, 1978.

Ford, Paul L., ed. *The Works of Thomas Jefferson.* Federal Edition, 12 vols. New York: G. P. Putnam's Sons, 1904.

Hutchinson, William T., William M. E. Rachal, Robert A. Rutland, and J. C. A. Stagg, eds. *The Papers of James Madison.* 17 vols. Chicago and Charlottesville: University Press of Virginia, 1962–91.

Jackson, Donald, and Dorothy Twohig, eds. *The Diaries of George Washington.* 6 vols. Charlottesville: University Press of Virginia, 1976–79.

Kerber, Linda K. *Federalists in Dissent: Imagery and Ideology in Jeffersonian America.* Ithaca: Cornell University Press, 1970.

Ketcham, Ralph. *James Madison: A Biography.* New York: Macmillan, 1971.

Ketcham, Ralph. *Presidents above Party: The First American Presidency, 1789–1829.* Chapel Hill: University of North Carolina Press, 1984.

Kohn, Richard H. *Eagle and Sword: The Federalists and the Creation of the Military Establishment in America, 1783–1802.* New York: Free Press, 1975.

Konig, David T., ed. *Devising Liberty: Preserving and Creating Freedom in the New American Republic.* Stanford: Stanford University Press, 1995.

Malone, Dumas. *Jefferson and His Time.* 6 vols. Boston: Little, Brown, 1948–81.

McCoy, Drew. *The Elusive Republic: Political Economy in Jeffersonian America.* Chapel Hill: University of North Carolina Press, 1980.

Matthews, Richard K. *The Radical Politics of Thomas Jefferson.* Lawrence: University Press of Kansas, 1984.

Miller, John C. *Alexander Hamilton and the Growth of the New Nation.* New York: Harper and Row, 1964.

Miller, John C. *The Federalist Era, 1789–1801.* New York: Harper and Brothers, 1960.

Mitchell, Broadus. *Alexander Hamilton: Youth to Maturity, 1755–1788.* New York: Macmillan, 1957.

Mitchell, Broadus. *Alexander Hamilton: The National Adventure, 1788–1804.* New York: Macmillan, 1962.

Peterson, Merrill D. *Thomas Jefferson and the New Nation: A Biography.* New York: Oxford University Press, 1970.

Prince, Carl E. *The Federalists and the Origins of the U.S. Civil Service.* New York: New York University Press, 1977.

Rossiter, Clinton. *Alexander Hamilton and the Constitution.* New York: Harcourt, Brace, and World, 1964.

Royster, Charles. *A Revolutionary People at War: The Continental Army and American National Character, 1775–1783.* Chapel Hill: University of North Carolina Press, 1979.

Sharp, James Roger. *American Politics in the Early Republic: The Nation in Crisis.* New Haven: Yale University Press, 1993.

Smelser, Marshall. *The Democratic Republic, 1801–1815.* New York: Harper and Row, 1968.

Smith, James Morton. *Freedom's Fetters: The Alien and Sedition Laws and American Civil Liberties.* Ithaca: Cornell University Press, 1956.

Smith, James Morton, ed. *The Republic of Letters: The Correspondence between Thomas Jefferson and James Madison, 1776–1826.* 3 vols. New York: W. W. Norton, 1995.

Syrett, Harold C., Jacob E. Cook, Barbara Chernow, and Patricia Syrett, eds. *The Papers of Alexander Hamilton.* 27 vols. New York: Columbia University Press, 1961–87.

Wood, Gordon W. *The Creation of the American Republic, 1776–1787.* Chapel Hill: University of North Carolina Press, 1969.

Index

181